A Quirk of Fate

Journey of a Carrot Top Black Boy

Monte Richardson

ISBN: 9780998167299

Library of Congress Control Number: 2017913243

Book layout and cover design by Robin Krauss, www.bookformatters.com
Photographs and illustrations by Monte Richardson.

Acknowledgements

I would like to express my sincere gratitude to my friends and family who have encouraged me along this journey of writing. I didn't know where it would take me, and while no blood, the sweat and tears rewarded me, unexpectedly. I especially thank my sister Valerie and my brother Chuck for their valuable help. And of course, my daughter Melody and son Orman, proud of the adults they are and the kids they were.

This book could not have happened without the editing and technical guidance of author Michelle Jackson, for whose long suffering assistance I am so thankful.

My deepest appreciation is for my wife, Birnur, for whom I dedicate this. Her persistence, her patience, her perspective, made me a real man, a real father, and now, a real author. Thank you, Birnur. I live for you.

Dedicated to my wife,

Birnur

The end of 2016 was a hopeful time for us, Birnur had accepted an early retirement package and was excited about becoming a translator. She had been hired numerous times by CNN and other companies, and believed she could maintain a steady but easy paced work life. I had just finished my final draft of this book and was excited about getting to the next steps of layout etc., We had also spent summer and fall getting me started in voice work, building a recording booth in our home and seeing a voice coach throughout those months.

In mid-December, after fighting a persistent cough for several weeks, Birnur was diagnosed with stage 4 lung cancer.

It was a brutal, advanced form with three mutations. Tests were done at the Mayo Clinic and the Foundation One laboratories to try to identify the mutations and their origins. Two, were not typical at all and doctors were not able to say where, or what organ, any of the cancers began.

At the end of April, 2017, I lost my love, my life in a very true way.

I struggled with the thought of adding this to the book; it was finished, how could I? However, how could I not. This has been the most profoundly painful, disbelieving, and fearful time of my life. I don't know what to say. I don't know how to think. I should not think I can possibly convey my thoughts so soon. After spending the last few years reflecting on my life, the quirks and ironies, and luck, it seemed to me I found some perspective. Suddenly, it is rendered premature. Birnur, defined my life. Her love for her family and friends, her deep concern for children, her commitment to me, is the real story. My name will always be, Birnur.

To share life so closely, so completely for almost 35 yrs., you really do become 'one'. Living, becomes a matter of dual consciousness, a reflexive consideration of your "better half" in virtually any thought. I have, now, a sad, angry desire to know death, too. I do not want to die, I just have an innate need to hold her hand, her mind, through this too. My other half most certainly still exist, it is only now unknowable.

I knew when I started this book I would dedicate it to Birnur, a thank you of sort for her love and sacrifice for me. I never dreamed that as I ended it, I would start the most heart-breaking chapter of my life. Birnur had many chapters taken from her; a relaxed retirement, grandchildren, long visits back home in Turkey, simply more time to share herself. She so deserved it. I said in this book that maybe things happen for our ultimate good, Man's ultimate good, simple evolution. Why do I now feel guilty for expressing that. Do we, in some subconscious thought vibrations, invite things to happen? Does evolution have a sense of irony?

Heraclitus, the ancient philosopher of Ephesus, the city only minutes from Birnur's home, Izmir, in Turkey, said "For God, all things are good and just, but for man some things are good and just and others are not." As a man, I can see nothing good or just about this. Hopefully, now, for Birnur, she can. Rest, sweetheart. Wait for me to share eternity, it is our fate.

I love you.

One

I sat at my desk that morning and went through the usual checks of emails and messages and engaged in small talk with my colleagues, primarily about politics and the pathetic situation with Iraq and President George W. Bush. The banter was light hearted, unlike the issues, and we tried to respect the position of those who still supported the decision to invade. Our office was like a million others around the country, a large room full of 6'x6' cubicles. In our case, the partitions were only about waist high, giving everyone seated a head and shoulder view of each other, something necessary in a major market TV newsroom. WXIA, the NBC affiliate in Atlanta, still had a family feel for me after twenty-five years. More than a dozen or so in the newsroom I had known that long, others for ten years or more, so morning chats could vary from kids to killers. Several reporters and photographers walked by briskly, grabbing video cassettes, scripts, and sometimes keys to one of our 'live' vans that they would be on-air from later that evening. About 9:45 my phone rang and I swung around and grabbed it, answering with the same greeting I would give ten times a day, "Morning, Call for Action." "Mr. Richardson, Dr. Curry, good morning" was the surprising voice on the line. I slowly slid my chair closer to the desk and felt a slight unease. Huddling the phone, I leaned forward as if I was being whispered to. "Hi, Dr. Curry, how are you?" I replied. I knew it had to be news about my earlier visit, and I began the long 'slow motion' second we live when we are about to get "the verdict" from our doctor. "Ok . . . listen, I need you to come in right now," he said. "Now?" You mean this minute?" I said. "Yes, need you to get in now, right now." His voice carried an urgency I'd never heard before. "What's up, something wrong?" I said, thinking of what I had told him in a visit two days earlier: "Something is not right." "We'll talk about it when you get here, just come on in. Go downstairs to the infusion clinic, we're gonna get some fluids in you." I put the phone down and sat still for a minute, weighing what all this meant for the rest of my work day and the rest of the story that was waiting for me. The seconds passed like minutes, but I didn't hesitate. I stood and walked over to a colleague and told her I had to leave. I must have had a very blank look on my face because she didn't question it. The sounds of the newsroom: phones ringing, police scanners blaring, conversations loud and soft were not there. It was surreal to say the least. I was aware of what I was saying and what was being said to me, but my mind was floating on what? . . . What is it?

I'm not the type that panics, but hearing the tone in Dr. Curry's voice was an echo that worried me. He had been my doctor for over ten years and was always easygoing and positive, but not this time. I turned and as I walked out I called my partner, Bill, the reporter I worked with each day in the 'Call for Action' unit at the station. He was pretty shocked and asked if I needed help, eager to do anything he could. Bill told me later that after my call he thought about something a public relations person had said to us a week earlier, "Wow, Monte, you are really losing weight." I told him I would be in touch, looking to the floor as the bland gray and maroon motif of the carpet tiles rolled under my feet, day dreaming, in a haze.

Walking to my car, I came upon my friend, Jennifer, in the garage. "Where you headed," she asked, thinking I was going out on assignment. "I'm actually going to my doctor . . . he told me to come in right away," I said. "What's wrong, you ok?" her eyes showed the look of concern as she asked. I told her I had no idea, that I had been feeling weird lately and went to him about it a few days ago. "Yeah, he just called me . . . I don't know . . . just said get in now." Jennifer looked at me a moment not saying anything. I could sense she was thinking what I was thinking . . . that's kind of scary, getting a call like that. "You have any idea? He didn't give you an idea?" "Not really." "Hope things are OK," she sighed. I turned away rather quickly as I felt a difficult welling in my eyes.

At the clinic, Dr. Curry told me I had a very high enzyme in my blood, that it could be from a couple of things, but at any rate, we needed to get fluids in me immediately to help flush it. "You need to check into a hospital, either now, this weekend, or first thing Monday," he said. "Your cpk is over

22,000, the normal is around 200, so we have to find out why," again his voice was anxious and I decided to go to the emergency room at Northside Hospital that afternoon. The cpk enzyme is a measure of muscle damage in the body; it can reflect heart problems, but that would usually show other symptoms.

"This is pretty extraordinary. We sometimes see this kind of level in pro football players after a game because of the intense battering their muscles receive" I was told by one doctor as I lay on the gurney waiting for the rheumatologist from my insurance company, Kaiser. Meanwhile, I was soon checked into a room. Other doctors came in and told me they wanted to do a biopsy on my right thigh, the weakest of my muscles, probably the next morning. So there I am, in the hospital, in a bed, nurses and doctors coming and going, taking blood and putting me on IVs. Birnur, my wife of over twenty years, sat with me. I don't think I had lost much of the blank look I'd had since I answered the phone that morning. We didn't feel worried necessarily, although it was obvious I had a problem. That afternoon my sister and brother stopped by, all of us surprised to find ourselves there, not for an injury or childbirth or even an illness you might expect, but something unknown. They offered the normal encouragements and assigned it to stress or perhaps a virus or maybe even alcohol damage to the muscles. I had done research on the internet about various diseases that caused muscle weakness, and while there were several possibilities, I did not have all the symptoms that would suggest one of them particularly. I felt uncomfortable with all the attention, not so much shyness, as the attention fed the already uncomfortable feeling I had lived with for several weeks, the feeling that something was not right. Feelings are often the best intelligence we have, when sensing if something is good or bad. It is our emotions about others, when you feel they are lying for example. We can even sometimes feel the answer to a problem that we cannot otherwise articulate. The feeling I had in those days was not wrong, I had a bizarre illness, one that was so rare and so difficult, that had I known how hard things would become, I may have felt helpless, perhaps hopeless.

As the days passed into weeks, and months into years, as I saw one expert after another, tried one medication or treatment after another, embraced the prayers and anecdotes of family and friends, and as I tried to reconcile the question of God and fairness, I slowly grew familiar again with an old feeling. For years I had lived a somewhat lucky life, seeing much of the world, having a beautiful wife and two beautiful children, meeting famous people and world leaders, and at times witnessing moments in life so raw it would leave me feeling guilty. Now, I was spending half the day mostly alone, with a frustration and anxiety that, after a short lifetime, had returned. I had lived through this before, an inescapable situation that burdened me every day with sporadic difficult efforts to get through the most casual times of childhood. I had asked why and how long as a child, the same questions I ask now in my fifties. I realize that in the context of life in this world I am not so much unlucky as just peculiar, like the young boy I was in the 1960s. God played a little trick on me then and, I hope decided I did well. Perhaps, He wants to watch again.

Azalea Mall was one of the first malls in Richmond, Virginia. It was small by today's standards, but still an enclosed playground of sort, where a fifteen-year-old could go to get a new pair of sneakers, rather than downtown at Thalhimers or Miller & Rhodes. Those large department stores were fun at times; we'd go there to ride the elevators and escalators, but Azalea Mall was close, close enough to walk. That made a difference when we didn't want to go through the trouble of catching the bus, which was fun in its own way, but after all just a bus. The new pair of sneakers I wanted were Converse basketball shoes, 'Chuck Taylor All Stars.' All Stars were necessary; it was The shoe that everyone wore. A pair would cost about ten dollars, which was not a small amount for us then, but if you had ten dollars, it was what you wanted first. I decided to take the walk, about a thirty-minute trek, one summer evening and buy a pair of white high-tops, with the prominent red star on the side. The white Converse were the most classy, with their clean red and black lines standing out against the white canvas top and gray soles; they made me feel just a touch older and "cool." A new pair of "Cons" was a big deal, and to get them myself, for the first time, was exciting. I didn't stay long at Azalea Mall that day, its long lone corridor had few kids my age, and I figured since it was getting late there wasn't much reason to linger. Still wearing my plain old Keds sneakers, I headed home with my new purchase swinging with my stride. The first quarter mile of that walk took me down Chamberlayne Ave., a broad, oak lined street of homes ranging from nice middle-class houses to some that were once true mansions; large stone or brick homes with columned porches, wide, tall front steps and multiple high chimneys. Chamberlayne Ave. was a mixture, a mixture of white and black folks, some of whom had lived there for decades, others maybe only days. The "white flight" of the sixties had left this once grand avenue of the thirties and forties not quite as elegant in 1971, but still very charming, the remnants of old southern elegance that, a century before, was the capital of the Confederacy.

The weather that evening was warm but not humid, perfect for walking, with the slow lingering light of summertime dusk and the winding high sirens of Cicada bugs blending with the "whoosh" of passing cars. I had to watch my step as I passed the large oak trees, sometimes-fragrant magnolias, in an effort not to trip on the erupting sidewalk resting across their roots. I imagined the ease of traversing those lumpy stretches with my new Cons. I was athletic, strong, and felt confident I would be more so in my new shoes hurdling a fence or climbing a tree. I gazed at the headlights and houses, often hearing the faint sounds of Marvin Gaye or The Temptations from a car or upstairs bedroom, which might draw my eyes as well. My route zigzagged through side streets where soon the blended neighborhood would give way to an all-black section of modest homes and apartment complexes. It was not my neighborhood but an area called Ginter Park, which bordered Providence Park, my destination. The Ginter Park School was the kind of school I always wanted to attend simply because of the structure. Built about a hundred years ago, it was large and majestic with brick and granite, deep green roof tiles and ornate wood, even stained glass over the entrance. It was built I'm sure, for the youngsters who once lived on that grand avenue I had just left.

Behind the school there was a playground, and of course, on the playground kids, playing basketball even as the dim evening light fouled their shots. I could hear the crisp jingle of the chain link nets, used to outlast the youngsters, and bouncing balls under their loud and laughing banter. With four or five courts, the rattling nets had a kind of "jingle bells" quality. I could only see shadows and shapes of young teenagers, about ten or fifteen of them, shooting around and talking shit, even though the night had ended any chance of a fair game. They were only silhouettes of afros and Converse using an invisible ball. I decided to cross the street and continue on a not as old, more level sidewalk. I looked straight ahead but my ears stayed with the balls and trash talk on those courts. After just a few seconds, the "jingle bells" and boisterous bragging ended. There was suddenly just hushed words between them, the sounds of Cicadas and cars in the distance now a sort of drum roll. I hoped for a moment or two, but, I could hear them; "Hey man, check it out—where da fuck he goin"— "Naw, fuck dat, come'on"— "Shiiid." The chorus built, and they urged themselves from the dark court and focused squarely on me. I walked to the base of a streetlight to slow and stop, knowing it would be wrong to run, especially in the dark. As they neared, my fear was complete when I realized they carried things. Chains and sticks swung with the motion of the group as they bounced on their toes and flexed their shoulders, enforcing the intent they had. The glisten of sweat jumped from one to the other while their soft chuckles terrified me. I knew why they were coming after me; I wasn't surprised, just afraid.

My blissful walk was now a near panic stand under the yellow glow of a streetlight as the pack of young men surrounded me. "Da fuck you doin' here" came from one in the group. I could not see well because I was directly under the light and had to squint to, hopefully, recognize someone. "Mafucka you mus be crazy, huh?" Their words blended taunts and questions that didn't permit a response, like the barks and growls of a wolf pack just before the last move. I stood still and tried to look at them as if we knew each other. "Yo, whas goin on?" I tried to say but, "Whe'da fuck you goin?" asked the one up front. "I'm going home, I'm just coming back from the mall," I said. "What's in d'bag?" another said. "Some shoes, just some shoes" as I raised the bag in a half-hearted gesture. The warm tingling sensation that precedes imminent danger filled my chest and skull. I didn't look away or at anything in particular but I could see the heavy chain one kid was drawing between his hands. It seemed I could see almost all of them, and everything they carried, at once. They rocked back and forth against each other shaking their arms like a sprinter just before he enters his blocks. "Fuck dat" one of them murmured, pushing forward. At that point I could only submit; the kind of release you give when falling, trying to roll into it, not to resist. It could not have been but moments before they would strike when a voice jumped from the rear, "Hold on man, hold on, be cool, he ain't white, Yo, he live over in Providence, I know him, he be hangin' out wit Fish'n 'em." I could not see him well; he was short and seemed to be one of the followers as opposed to a leader. There was a long single second of silence and hope. "O yeah, yeah I know dat dude" came from another in the shadows. The entire gang swayed back like a strong breeze had snuck up on them. In seconds, as if the breeze was a magic gas, the wolves had become lambs as their shoulders relaxed and heads tilted. Now, seconds later, they were jiving with someone they knew. "Damn, you ain't white?," one at the front asked. He reached out and touched my hair and laughed saying "shit, I know I seen it all now."

They chuckled at me as if we were all ten year olds and I had dropped my ice cream, teasing my misfortune. A couple of them raised their hands to give me five and the handshake brothers used known as "the dap." They told me of their friend that had been attacked in the white neighborhood not far away. "Yeah, we were gonna fuck-you-up, send yo ass back witta message . . . ah haha." Their chains and sticks soon swung loosely, even playfully. I felt the air return to my lungs, and my nervous smile grew more genuine. We talked a little about 'Fish' and others from Providence Park; then, we checked out my new Cons . . . "yeh, you alright."

Only a few minutes after they spotted me they were slowly raising the laugh and lip levels back to normal. "Shiid, he woulda probley whip yo ass, nigga," one said to another causing a loud laugh to roll over them. They pushed at each other laughing and teasing while they returned to the dark courts to continue as if nothing had happened. I stood still, breathing heavily, almost wanting to laugh myself. I went back to a more earnest stroll, relaxed, but angered by my recurring burden . . . feeling lucky, to be lucky, this time. I didn't hear the Cicadas or cars, or think about hopping fences, I only clutched my bag tightly and wondered why, as I often did, I had to be so "lucky." The closer I got to home and the area where I was a familiar sight, the more I hummed Marvin Gaye again.

When I made it home I didn't mention anything to my mom, I just showed her my new shoes. "They sho cost enough. I hope they last you" she said, not knowing how fortunate it was that they had lasted the walk home. I asked if I could have some ice cream and watch TV. "I guess that's alright" she whispered while leaving the kitchen. It wasn't long before I was enjoying the TV and ice cream, not necessarily feeling any post event stress like you might after escaping a bad accident. By now, at fifteen, I was getting used to that kind of situation, if not that kind of luck.

That one evening, for many years, gave me belief that there might be Divine intervention at times, that God, or at least miracles, are possible. I didn't know anyone in that gang of teenagers, least of whom the source of my salvation, he never came forward to see me face to face, a kind of anonymous angel. It is harder to think it was just random luck, not because of the notion of luck, but the concept of random. I guess considering all that happened that evening, in that place, it was normal. My place, and my time, was in Richmond, Virginia, at the crest of the civil rights movement. A time and place where what happened was always seen through a filter of prejudice, from virtually everyone, black or white. However, in another place or time they may have seen me as just another kid going down the street. Place and time, a random spot we inherit. Where and when is the real luck. The year 1971 pushed at the social and racial identities of both generations, challenging fixed perceptions about almost everything, even truth. It typified my world growing up, dealing with the perceptions of others, their reality vs. mine. And all too often, my reality was shaped by their perception.

Two

Our family histories are hard to know because for so many black families in America there is so little record. The vast records of white life nourish the curious Caucasian, who would lay claim to have "come over on the Mayflower." But alas, poor Leroy, he knows not his name. I know that my father's father was a chauffeur for a prominent Richmond doctor, but I know little of his parents, and nothing beyond them. On my paternal grandmother's side, I know more, in fact back to a slave named Frederick Greene. On mother's side there is a little more, a generation or two, that my grandparents were what was called 'Mulatto' in the census records. That would indicate there was white blood, but hardly a chance to know its source. I was told my great-great grandfather was from Ireland, but my mom was not sure. The rich tradition of the "Griot," or history, handed down through story can be invaluable if the family has it, but it can be only as meaningful as the face which tells it. But there is something potent in viewing the written marks of hands that were there, even if it describes the sale of a relative or the notice of his death. This lack of official witness, if you will, has left the bloodline of African Americans a very complex and ambiguous tale.

The laws of the land dictated that any black made you all black, that white had to be pure, purged of any putrid mix. The irony that the white population is, likely, just as mixed will have to fascinate future historians. It is certainly undeniable the tremendous role Black Americans have played in making our great cultural and economic power, but they were roles of great individuals that made history. The history of a given family is a much different story. Yes, we know that some of our great-great-great grandparents were slaves, and that their parents too, lived entire lives in absolute service. We knew of ourselves only by the names and narratives dictated upon us. When Barack Obama was elected the first black president, I thought it was so poignant, so historically poetic; he did not have a slave name. There is no Johnson, Washington, or Roosevelt in that office. It is indeed, a true "Black" name on the desk, as if Africa would not be denied the respect that had been denied Africans in America.

Our family lived in a home my grandfather built in the 1920s. It was very close to a landfill, what we used to call "the dump." My dad, Charles Hoover Richardson, worked hard to make it a nice home. Even though it was without running water, our water drawn from a well, it was respectful. We had a nice lawn and garden, a circle gravel driveway, lots of little touches that let you know he was proud of his home. He would always say "If something is worth doing at all, it's worth doing right." He was never afraid of work and never afraid to put us to it as well. And 'us' was more than a few. By the time my father was thirty he had six children, ultimately eight. He and my mother, Cora Ruth Feggins, were married at eighteen. Back then I don't think that was unusual, but to support and raise such a family was an effort that really defined my parents. The early years were very tough, tough for any black family in the early fifties, but when you have only a ninth-grade education and the need for the mother to be home with so many mouths to feed and nurture . . . well. Nevertheless, from such an early start they met the responsibility and fulfilled it for 56 years.

I was born to them in 1956. It was like the scene in the Steve Martin movie "The Jerk". . ."I was born a poor black child," went one of the opening lines. I was like everyone else, only different. A poor black child in a section called Church Hill, on the east side of Richmond. Like many black communities around the south, Church Hill had all types of personalities that left no lack for gossip. It's an historic area, most notable for St. Johns Church, where, a couple hundred years ago a young man expressed a desire for freedom that became one of the most definitive statements of the American story, "Give me liberty or give me death." Seventy years later another Virginian would hold that ideal and act on it. However, Nat Turner was no Patrick Henry, but a slave that truly preferred death. His method was sad and brutal, but his passion for liberty went beyond words. But as we know, words, more often than action, can control our image of history. George Washington is probably the first good example of our historical editing. We were taught Washington was so virtuous that as a child he could not tell a lie. "Father, I cannot tell a lie, I chopped down the cherry tree" went the story that exalts the father of our country. But apparently so virtuous was our founder, he could not resist buying and selling human beings, including children. And the fact that his victory at Yorktown was owed to efforts of a slave, James Armistead Lafayette, who as a spy provided information key to the victory, is virtually unknown. Not to mention, poor Lafayette was returned to his master after securing the revolution that created America.

'Ford Avenue' was the name of our home in Church Hill, like Monticello or Mt. Vernon, it was our home's name. We lived there until I was four, any memories I have of these years are dreamlike snapshots, almost like imagining it happened. Like the time my dad prepared homemade ice cream. He had an old hand churner that he and my older brothers would crank slowly. "Vanilla is the best" he'd say, as if we could have another flavor. Other ingredients were out of the question. Churning the round wooden tub was fun for us and my dad. It's funny to remember your father as a very young man, like it was a different man. I can imagine him as a friend and the things he would talk about, his common-sense reflections on things. He may have lacked formal education, but like my mom, could be very analytical. They could always put things in context, never needing to use the 'sour grapes' excuse.

I remember my red tricycle and my younger sister, Vicki, she was barely able to walk and I would let her sit on it as I guided it. One morning I guided her into a cinder block wall under the stairs out back. I can still see the red, bloody, peeled back fingernail. I tried to comfort her as my mother would. Even at five, we know at least to mimic the actions of our parents when we are unsure. That couldn't stop the screams and tears that would bring my mother rushing down the stairs "Don't worry shugga, it's gonna be alright," she said calmly. My mom did what she had been doing for over 10 years at that point, handling the big and small emergencies of a family. They wrapped Vicki's finger and headed to the doctor. I felt sorry for my sister but, oddly, not guilty. It seemed that little red tricycle was to blame.

I remember the day in 1960 when we bought a new (used) car, daddy and my two older brothers sat at our big yellow kitchen table talking about what kind of car to buy. "What should I get, what do you think Chuck? What about you Butch?" My brothers shouted out names like "Chevrolet!" and "Cadillac!" At the time, my dad had a beautiful 1948 Pontiac, two tone green with chrome bumpers and a grille that wore like a championship belt. A new car was one of the most exciting things we could imagine. Of course, my dad had already determined what he was getting, but we all enjoyed the thrill of choosing. When dad was ready to go he said he would only take me. My brothers were mad and couldn't understand why he would not allow them to come after such hype. Years later I understood why, why he only took me. At that time and place, it helped to have me along. I suppose it could help one's credit rating, so to speak, to have a bright, freckle faced little redhead at the end of your arm.

We lived in Church Hill until 1961 when my father was told by the city "it needs Ford Avenue." It needed the land for an important project, a development he was told. He was told about eminent domain, a way the city could take your property. Oh, they would compensate you, but it was nothing considering the work he had put into it. It had so much more value than their appraisal. To the city, it was just an old two-story structure on an acre and a half of land, occupied by a black family in a black neighborhood . . . nothing special. I do not know for sure, but I would guess it was just a developer with connections at city hall who wanted to build public housing, 'projects,' because that's what happened. It was tough for us; this place was a diamond in the rough, an example of my father and his father's character. Things were somewhat worsened by the fact that the few thousand dollars from the city had to be divided among his siblings, four sisters, because it was deeded to the children of Charlie Richardson, my grandfather. My dad had put in all the labor to improve it, and paid the taxes, but now, had to split the money. His family of six children had to find a new place to remember as home.

We moved to one called 'Moss Side Avenue' in the early fall of 1961, in a house owned by Mrs. Sarah Eaton, a friend of my father's mother, who somehow made room for these eight people. Moss Side Avenue was in Battery Park, a working-class black neighborhood of folk who earned a decent living like teachers and postmen. There was a park at the end of street, with tennis courts maintained by Mr. Ashe, whose son, Arthur, had learned to play on a few years earlier. Arthur Ashe would go on to stardom, winning three 'Grand Slams' and becoming an internationally beloved humanitarian.

"Don't be afraid, you can do it, they will be real nice friends before you know it," she said. I started school that year at Norrell Elementary, I cried a bit before walking in, but Mama was right, it didn't take long. One good friend walked home with me every day, a friend named Aaron. We lived on opposite sides of the park so our route home would be across the park from each other. As we strolled the length of the courts and playgrounds throwing acorns and small sticks, we'd yell out to each other, "See ya later alligata."— "afta while crocodile". We were probably only fifty yards apart but with trees and the fence around the courts it seemed I was yelling to the other side of the world. I can only wonder what happened to Aaron, one of my first friends. I think realizing your first friendship is the first step of growing up, accepting the first person outside the immediate family, the first 'other.'

My two older brothers made friends quickly, often playing football directly across the street from our home. The large grassy area was part of church property, a Baptist church like many in Richmond. One afternoon while I stood around watching the young teens toss and tumble, I noticed the high iron fire escape that climbed the side of the three level church. From the street, it only appeared to have two floors, but the property sloped from the street with a basement, and was much taller from the rear. I have always enjoyed climbing, even into my adulthood, and so I took to the stairs to reach a birds-eye view of the game. It was fun and easy reaching the top, coming down however, was a challenge I didn't expect. When I looked at the steps dropping steeply before me I didn't realize they were likely designed to be descended backwards for balance, and help to those with a fear of heights. I took my first step, my only step, and went straight through the rail. I can still see my foot missing that first step. My brothers said I looked like a rag doll falling and flailing the twenty or so feet to the ground. I hit the ground hard, but I landed on my side not even knocking the wind out of me. My only pain was in my wrist that had been under my waist, badly bruised but no real injury. They say a child's body is resilient, kind of rubber-like I suppose, because my brothers would laugh later that day at how I "bounced". There was no laughter from my mother, who bounced her hand off their heads for not paying attention to me, lucky me.

———◆———

In 1963, we moved to Providence Park. My parents had worked and saved to build our small two bedroom one bath home in Henrico County. The lower middle-class neighborhood had a playground nearby, a little market a short walk away, and a small wooded area surrounding our house, which would provide so much for me until it fell victim to development in 1970 ... apartments. I'd become very familiar with the community around Ladies Mile Road. Ladies Mile Road, what a name, we always wondered about that. Providence Park seemed a fitting name, because there were a couple times when it indeed seemed 'Providence' was at work. When we moved there they were building a brand new structure and sanctuary for the Providence Park Baptist Church, which was literally a stone's throw away from our house. However, we never attended, as my mother was a member of the Mt. Tabor Baptist Church on the other side of town in Church Hill. She had been there for years and was the lead singer in the choir, having a beautiful voice. I don't attend church today, or often hear church music, but I still get choked up when I hear Mahalia Jackson's "Precious Lord, take my Hand," or "It is well with my Soul" as I see my mother singing, looking toward the heavens.

Providence Park gave me the experiences that flood the memory of childhood. All the laughter and sweat, the close calls on bikes or with bullies, but it was one of the first memories there that would, in hindsight, be a profound indication of experiences to come. Lots of kids would gather at a playground a short walk down the street and around the corner, it was on such a walk to the playground when that first odd thing occurred. It was a bright sunny afternoon in late spring. I think it was just after school because people were still at work, except most mothers. Shortly after I started, a police car rolled by then slowed and stopped. The two officers inside watched me walk by then inched up behind as if to follow. After a moment or so, one of the officers got out and called to me. "Hey son, where you going?" he asked. "Just to the playground" I said. I was not sure what to think, I didn't know if I was doing something wrong or if the playground was closed or what. At that time, it was not unusual to see small kids walking on the sidewalk going to the home of a friend or relative, certainly not toddlers, but I was about seven. "Where do you live?" was the next question. "Right up there" I said. "Up where?" he said, "Up there, right up there" I said. The officer was very nice and friendly but asked again "You live right up there?" "Yes, in that house right there" I said, as I pointed right at my home, not 100 yards away. "No, you don't live there son, you must be lost, you should come with us" he said.

His partner in the car was on the radio, "Unit 25, request a 10-20 . . . ," like something on TV but I don't recall what he actually said, just the officer in the car with the mic in his hand. I told the officer I had two brothers and three sisters and we went to Laburnum Elementary, he smiled and acted like I was confused. He put his hand on my shoulder and walked me to the car. I remember the big black shiny utility belt, the patent leather reflecting the bright sun making it seem wet-like, and the large handle of his gun poking high on his waist. I wasn't afraid, just fascinated with the close up encounter of a police uniform I had only seen on TV. "What's your name son?" he said, his words soft, as if to comfort. "Monte," I told him. "Don't worry, Monte, you're not in trouble, we just need to figure out where to take you." Like so many memories from childhood, they are snapshots of words and images, but that was the basic event. It was not long before I was in the car on the way to the police station, snatched off the street like a stray dog.

Fortunately, there were ladies, on Ladies Mile, mothers who saw all the kids on the block as their kids. One of my 'other mothers' had been looking out the window, I believe it was Mrs. Davis, checking on her kids, who saw the policeman talking to me and putting me in the car. She would alert my mom before the officers were much more than a block away. As a parent, today, I think of what my mother would have gone through if Mrs. Davis had not been there; the desperate and traumatic search, then finally, calling the police. She told me years later that she was so upset, but really couldn't blame the officers, "they were really only trying to rescue you" she said. Those policemen were rescuing a poor little white boy who had wandered onto the other side of the tracks into the "colored" neighborhood. I was saved yet stolen by the officers. Light-skinned blacks were not that unusual, but to see me was to look at a little red-headed cracker. Mama understood, you see, because my mom was almost as light-skinned as me, almost . . . because nobody was as light-skinned as me. I was white, paper white, red-headed white, easy to burn white. I was whiter than most Whites were. I was damned white. White enough that my mother would have to have my birth certificate corrected. They too, had only observed the obvious.

Understanding what happened that day was the beginning of a self-awareness that would be present in my psyche each day, to this day. It has been the source of profound insight, deep frustration, and a thousand challenges one person at a time, mostly painful yet some rewarding. The translucent story of America's blended ancestry is apparent in people like me but like real estate, it's about location, location in time, an American season.

My dad, Charles Hoover and me, Hoover LaMonte in 1957.

Three

Bracey, Virginia where my mother was born, is close to the North Carolina border in deep tobacco country. It can be dry and hot in the summer, a place in my memory of a beating sun and oven-like heat. The home was out in the country, where a neighbor might be a quarter mile away. We would visit her aunts, cousins, and old folk that seemed so, so old to me then. Everything seemed old there. It seemed even the earth itself was older, certainly that house was. The wood board structure was dry and cracked, deeply grayed from sun and time, well over a hundred years. With screen doors and rock footings to keep it above the dusty ground, flies and wasp were a constant challenge. I remember the large expanse of open field around the house and the pigs and cows. I could see in my relatives the invariable strain of white that surfaced. In some, it was enough to make them seem Middle Eastern or Mexican, in others hardly a clue. Those relatives too, were descended from a man named Robert Feggins, or from the Boyd family. In that small area of Mecklenburg County, it would seem everyone was of Feggins or Boyd decent. On census records a hundred years ago virtually everyone in that district was considered and marked on the census "mulatto:" mixed-race. My great grandfather Robert Feggins, some said, had Irish blood, which was one source of all the shades of skin that would reach their pale peak in me.

There were sometimes, usually unspoken, feelings of jealousy of the lighter skinned by some of the darker relatives, not of those that looked totally white like me, but of those with the fine hair and light brown skin. There too, I might be at the end of jokes and teases, not mean hearted, in fact loving, but still poignant. In that old home in Bracey, where the water was pumped by hand from a well, single light bulbs swung from the ceilings, where great age was seen wherever the eye fell, I sensed those families before me, roots. I knew this was where my mother, her mother, and her mother came from. Those unseen, albeit apparent, mix of black and white roots is not rare just officially forgotten. Although mixed race is as American as baseball, the separation was no game. It left us understanding that to be black was to be unpredictable like the weather, yet, like the seasons, we felt a certain comfort and appreciation in the distinct identity. I can only imagine the true extent through the last four hundred years. Whether W.E.B. Dubois, or the Seminole Indians, the rich mulatto story exists but a subtext of black life. Our roots were of a very mixed soil, but by default we grew under a black sun.

Back home, oatmeal was not the most delectable of breakfast options, but it was usually the only option. Mornings were often a struggle if we had school. I never liked getting up and getting ready early, especially for school. I didn't dread it, it was just the whole discipline and responsibility thing most kids avoid. I did not realize at the time the responsibility on my dad's shoulders. Hoover, as my mom called him, must have felt more than just responsibility as he worked two jobs my entire childhood. He would be up before me in the morning and home after I went to bed at night. The day's only relief, in the mid–afternoon, was when he came home for a nap and dinner, then off to his evening job. It can't be overstated what that said about the resolute nature of my dad. There were many afternoon dinners at our simple metal table with the yellow top. It was where we sat for all our meals, and where, on many afternoons, we were gazed upon. My father would sit across from us while Momma stood and cooked or cleaned the kitchen. My sister, Vicki, and I would glance at each other every few seconds wondering . . . what is he doing? Why is he looking at us? "Eat your peas, do you want some mashed potatoes?" my mother might say, but we would hold our giggle and try not to look back at daddy. Hoover would smell of fresh Aqua Velva and Alberto VO5, having his meal as he marveled at his two delightful creations across the table. Daddy would not necessarily stare, but he would be almost grinning as he studied us. "What's going on?" was the unspoken question bouncing between my sister and me. It was the kind of attention we didn't understand . . . at the time. That attention was a hint of what enabled my dad for so many years. It was, in a way I guess, the fuel that kept him focused on the responsibilities he would fulfill for decades.

"Guess I better hit the road" daddy mumbled as he rose to leave. Mama wiped her hands on her thin cotton apron and looked as if it was not something she wanted but it was all right. The sharp fall light held its place through the kitchen door as daddy stood and reached on top of the refrigerator for his keys. Always a quiet goodbye, he would glance at us and head out to his job at Richfood, a manufacturer of dairy products. I was never sure what exactly he did there, it is likely he cleaned or oversaw some cleaning team. Imagine today, six children in a home, it is more amazing than anything I could do. My father was a good man, he sacrificed all but his Sunday afternoons making and maintaining a home and yard for his family. While he wasn't there those times to assist with school or other things, he provided the means that allowed my mother to raise and nurture us. Daddy worked for the city of Richmond in the morning, collecting trash from the curbside of homes he could not even dream to have. When I see the sanitation workers grabbing my cans and bags today, I often think of my own dad and those many thousands of times he did the same as I slept. Charles Hoover Richardson, without a high school diploma, eventually worked his way to supervisor, after decades of those cans, working well over fifty years for the city. My father in fact holds the record as longest serving employee for the city of Richmond, fifty-three years. I guess it was what he had to do, and we are all very proud.

We are eight children. Over the course of forty years my parents raised Charles (Butch), Chuck, Valerie, Ruth, Vicki, Monte, Robert and Rick. Eight kids, all of us reaching adulthood basically OK. My mother would often say how blessed she was to have her children do so. Twenty years separated the first son from the youngest, so by the time the last two were born, the first two were out. It was a tight fit, a small, two-bedroom house with a kitchen and one bath. There were eight people, three boys in one bedroom, momma and daddy in another and three girls in what was the tiny dinning room. It was like having guest staying, sleeping in the open, on twin beds, but it wasn't, it was the girl's bedroom. All of this filled the needs of teenagers and toddlers, and thirty-somethings.

Evenings without daddy were as normal as momma's humming or

singing as she went about things. Ruth had strong faith, and with such, a view of life that would never leave her too fearful of tomorrow, concerned perhaps, but never truly fearful. A belief in Providence that what happens is supposed to happen for our ultimate good, guided her. We were used to the soft hum or singing that shared the sound of pots and pans and the baiting smell of her meals. The singing seemed to express a comfort with life however difficult. She certainly was no Pollyanna but did seem to have a sort of innate happiness. It was a trait that everyone would always recognize in "Momma Ruth." For a child to sense that in his mother is lucky, indeed precious. But my mom was also tough and practical. "If you don't get in there and finish what I told you your butt's gonna go to bed so fast your head's gonna swim!" momma might say without haste. That happiness was always lined with 'tough love.' Raising five or six children, she had to manage them as well as love and nurture them. Around seven-thirty or eight we would be able to watch TV for a while, shows like 'Laugh In' or 'Get Smart'. Momma would continue with ironing or sewing, or working on one of her Afghans, slowly knitting the colors together to make one of the large throws that would adorn the couches and beds of all our homes in the years ahead. "That's so silly" she'd say as a small rumble of laughter rose from her belly, referring to the television she was not watching but listening to.

When we moved to that new home in Providence Park, she insisted we go to the closest school, a white school. The black school was almost ten miles away. This was just months after the Cuban missile crisis and she was "not going to have my children any further from me than necessary," she told others. There was also the time she fought for the job my sister Valerie got at the C&P phone company when in high school. Valerie had been denied a couple times, being told there were no openings, while other white kids at Henrico High school, not nearly the academic, involved achiever Valerie was, were being hired easily. I don't know if she went down there and presented herself as white or not, but she won Valerie the job. For a few years in the sixties, my mom worked at the Central National Bank in Richmond as a bookkeeper. It was a job almost unheard of for black women. Momma later in life said it was an early version of 'don't ask don't tell'. . ."they didn't ask and I didn't tell, sometimes it could be handy," she would grin thinking about it and laugh.

So as daddy spent his evenings without us and the homework, or 'Laugh In', he, and momma, did what they had to do. Hoover didn't have time for much recreation but he enjoyed music, the big bands, Frank Sinatra, and Bossa Nova. He owned a guitar, an electric 'Silvertone,' black and shinny. It disappeared at Christmas, in 1965, when someone broke into our home. All our wrapped gifts were stolen and daddy's guitar. We didn't mind so much about the gifts, but we could tell it hurt him to lose his guitar. Later, his free time was spent watching pro baseball or westerns on TV. Mostly, when he was not at work, he was at work at home. Charles Hoover was, as they say, a jack of all trades. In our neighborhood, there was no such thing as hiring someone to fix plumbing or paint the house, much less keep the lawn cut. It was the case for lots poor people who had to "do it themselves," but he made it a point to involve us, again necessity, but also to instill self-reliance. "You gonna let that little piece of metal beat you . . . it's just metal . . . you have a brain." I would hear words like that often whenever I had problems with a task. We did it all, and our mind we learned, was our most valuable tool. We maintained and improved that home in Providence, often teased by friends for the chores that always slowed us from play. Those hours of learning hands-on how to maintain a house, yard, and cars, can't be measured against the thousands of dollars saved on our own homes over the years.

One of the most nicely kept homes was our neighbor's. It was a two-story white stucco with a large front porch and a perfectly manicured lawn. Built back in the twenties when the area was mostly woods and gravel roads, it almost seemed out of place, like a mistake. A fairly large house, for the area, it faced a section of woods, not any road. It was at the end of a driveway— more than a road, to the rear of the church, basically sitting in the back of the homes on Ladies Mile Road. The owner, Mr. Woolfolk, did all the work on this unique house with large window awnings and a white, single-rail fence. There was no furnace or A/C, just a wood burning stove and window fans. Red and white rose plants at the yard corners emphasized the pride and care taken for the home. Even the front porch was kept freshly painted, with hanging plants and old wooden lawn chairs facing the trees. It had "curb appeal" without a curb. They appealed purely to Mr. Woolfolk. I would see him sometimes from our house, down on his hands and knees feeling about the grass as if he had dropped something. We knew he could lose things but what he was usually looking for on the ground was imperfection, flaws, found by hand. That immaculate yard was the home of a blind man. Mr. Woolfolk had slowly gone blind as an adult, and now in his late fifties, could only see light and some colors. He would spend hours sometimes going over an area he had been over several times, but he seemed never daunted by possible futility. I would help him often with things he needed, including sometimes just my company, and eyes.

Mrs. Woolfolk would be in the house, but I rarely saw her. They had a somewhat antagonistic relationship; any talking was more of a shout at each other. It was funny because he was always a happy and jovial person, despite the burden and pain of losing his sight. He was never afraid of work even with such limits. He boasted the fact he could get things done. "All you need is common sense and mother wit," he'd say with a broad upward grin. Gilbert, his first name, was always cheerful and talkative. He liked to show us his hands, "That's a workin' man's hands" he would say. Indeed, his hands were like none I have ever seen to this day. They worked many years in construction labor with brick and cement, and now endured the perils of blind direction. They were hard with calluses and healed wounds. The sections of his fingers were block-like, making his hands look almost ceramic, as if the wear had been baked in. It's weird and, for me now, somewhat sad, that I'll never forget what he looked like, yet, Mr. Woolfolk never really saw my face. I remember a lot from him, that physical labor is not without value or pride, that common sense and mother wit made anything possible, and probably of most value, as an adult, that perseverance of the spirit is what counts in *any* darkness.

One of the things I like about Richmond is the distinct change in seasons, a beautiful spring, hot summer, crisp falls with deep blue skies, often with what they call an Indian summer, and a winter that requires a good coat for the snow that was usually enough to enjoy but not necessarily a constant problem. The changes seem to give better definition of time in memories as well. By the summer of 1965, we had lived in Providence Park about two years and Richmond was celebrating the centennial of the Civil War. I remember the Confederate flags and the museum downtown that was dedicated to the past, a past when Richmond was the capital of the Confederacy, the capital of Virginia. Virginia was what many called the "mother of slavery" as it related to the U.S. Virginia supplied a huge portion of the trade the last fifty years of slavery, the result of almost two hundred years of basically breeding humans for not only labor but trade. There weren't breeding farms as such, but it was very much an element of plantation or farm management. Slaves were as much capital as any piece of gold or silver, so a child was interest added to the asset column. In 1857 alone, Richmond moved this 'capital' to the tune of close to half a billion of today's dollars—look it up.

Virginia, in no small measure, held its heritage closely. I remember the gleaming statues on Monument Ave. There, at the dawn of the twentieth century, they erected a series of monuments to honor confederate heroes like Robert E. Lee, Stonewall Jackson, Jefferson Davis and J.E.B. Stuart. They would rise up every few blocks at the major intersections, grand forty-foot high symbols of the Confederacy, most on horseback in full regalia, resolute in their cause. They said if the rider was facing north he died in battle, south if after the war. It was a summer that would celebrate battles won and lost at places with names like Manassas and Seven Pines and, less so, a town named Appomattox. Richmond in the sixties was a place of confederate license plates, stock car racing, and the home of Marlboro cigarettes . . . Phillip Morris. In those days, the Civil War was not just history but, for many, an ongoing cause. A pride in what they saw as a prim society of honor and grace and brave men who died to protect it. Southerners, as James Baldwin described, clung to two antithetical doctrines: A pride in America and the beliefs and principles of the Constitution, proud citizens of a free society. On the other hand, sentimental and loyal to a society which had been destroyed by those principles. Many were unwilling to concede, much less come to terms with its brutal legacy.

Today, in cities and towns around the South, not the least Richmond, there is a slow movement to address the presence of monuments to the confederacy and its leaders. In endless town squares throughout Georgia, North Carolina, Mississippi, Alabama, South Carolina, Virginia, you name the state in the Confederacy, there is the noble southern rebel soldier atop its pedestal in the heart of the town. The grand displays like that at Stone Mountain near Atlanta or in Richmond represent hundreds of little tributes from county seats to university centers. There is a growing question: are they offensive? Whenever I discuss it with those who are uncertain, or worse yet, indifferent, I ask a simple question. Why do you think there are no confederate monuments in Ohio or Pennsylvania or New York or Massachusetts, what would be the reaction of those citizens, white or black, at such a notion? The answer is obvious, they were the enemy, they killed our forefathers, they were traitors, why would they honor such monuments in the center of, say Philadelphia? It's so easily understandable. But, millions of black citizens throughout the south are expected to acknowledge and even pay for the preservation of symbols of an enemy many times over that perceived by the union descendants in Gettysburg, Pa.

For many whites that are my age and older who carried such genuine pride in those men on horseback, it must be pretty unnerving to see that "colored" man as president . . . a guilt-driven paranoia that most would deny with the stubborn indignant glare of Stonewall Jackson. As a child, you really don't understand the world beyond its face value. I saw those statues and flags and celebrations as just that. I knew how color was a big issue for me, big for Richmond, but I didn't really connect Civil War and slavery to it; it was just so long ago.

It was, ironically, also a time of integration in schools and public places. In fact, my family was one of only three families to integrate Henrico High School and Laburnum Elementary earlier in 1963. That first week following the 'March on Washington,' county schools around Richmond began admitting blacks. As I remember, my sister, Ruthie, and I were the only ones at the elementary, she in the sixth grade and me in the second. My three older siblings, a sister and two brothers, were the first to attend the high school, they and two other black students among almost 1000. That fall, as word went out that there were "negroes" on campus, all eyes fell in search.

Linda Brown, one of them, was hard to miss, a very attractive brown skin girl, she resembled the singer Nancy Wilson. She, like others of that decade, had to accept the brunt of hostility and disdain for being the first to integrate. My brothers and sister were less conspicuous until you got up close. Nonetheless, they were subject to intense, and at times, violent receptions. My brother, Chuck, had his locker set on fire, my brother Butch was chased from the football field by the opposing team during a game! My sister Valerie would have to endure constant snickers and remarks like "I'm not sitting next to the nigger." Butch recalls the day President Kennedy was shot. "They announced on the speaker in the classroom that Kennedy had been shot, and several kids jumped and said, yeah!" It was not quite as rough in the elementary for my sister Ruthie and me; the more obvious reactions were from the teachers and staff than the kids. We did not look Black. It was only from word of mouth that the slow change in the eyes and actions of our classmates let us know they knew. It's hard to believe how many Virginians felt then, many Americans for that matter, but saddening to realize how steeped in resentment and hatred the South was.

"Let's sing "Dixie!" Who knows "Dixie?" shouted Mrs. Maddox, my fifth-grade teacher. It was early in the school year, and as we started each morning, we pledged allegiance to the flag and sang 'God Bless America'. On this morning, Mrs. Maddox felt we should honor a special part of America. "Who knows "Dixie," show me your hands?" she said enthusiastically. Less than half the class raised their hands as we gazed at each other. Of course we had all heard the song, and for a moment, we tried to race it through our minds and recall the words. When only a few hands remained up, Mrs. Maddox was shocked. Her mouth dropped and she had a look as if thinking "you poor children." "You don't know 'Dixie'. . . you ought to be ashamed!" she said with a very southern drawl that was so appropriate for her dismay. She stood for a moment, eyes crossing over us as if she was looking for a thief. "Well, we are gonna learn today" she said as she turned to her desk and put down the chalk and book she held. Mrs. Maddox was indeed a so-called southern belle. Young, perhaps in her late twenties, she was very attractive with premeditative charm. She wore a mild version of the 'beehive,' the iconic hairstyle of southern women, blonde, naturally. From a small town in Mississippi, "Dixie" was dear to her heart. "Raymond, just south of Jackson" she would proudly proclaim. "You know, just south of where we shot Medgar Evers in the back in his driveway a couple years ago . . . hee, hee, hee." She didn't actually say that, but I doubt she and others from Raymond lost much sleep over his murder. She held a clear reverence for "Dixie," the song and the place.

So now, her lesson for the day was to instill a bit of that reverence in us. We did no reading, writing, or arithmetic until we knew "Dixie." Old times there are not forgotten. Any slavery thoughts were reconciled as just part of "old times." "It was just the times; it was just how people were." It was a time known as the age of enlightenment throughout Europe, the times of Voltaire, Rousseau, and even here, Thomas Paine and Jefferson, a time when men tried to think about themselves and others rationally, even if not modestly. Unfortunately, here in America, perhaps because of the vast geography, the convergence and conveyance of any enlightenment was minimal. "Dixie" was so averse to enlightenment it would maintain the enslavement of literally half its people, conveniently. After all, there was gold in half those people. In 1860, Mississippi was home to more millionaires than any other state, their fortunes held in Black gold. The thought of those dollars simply being set free must have been absurd.

They chose, basically, to ignore the light. Like Mark Twain said, "It ain't what you don't know that will hurt you, it's what you know for sure that ain't so." While Mrs. Maddox made us remember that song with her gleeful daydreams about things that ain't so, today, she must be profoundly despondent to see that a black mayor, Chokwe Lumumba, once a proponent of a "New Africa" in the South, would lead her capital city of Jackson.

Four

Soon, this 'race' thing started to persuade the way I would maneuver and shield myself. When you are ten years old, you have a natural shyness and tendencies of caution in social situations. I had to start getting used to that inevitable moment, the moment when this friend, or that teacher, or even a whole class, would give me 'the look.' The look would sometimes be just quizzical, sometimes disbelief like Mrs. Maddox over a song, sometimes triggering anger as if betrayed. It was usually not something the kids would dwell on, it was curious, but not something that would get in the way of play . . . very little got in the way of playing dodge ball, kick ball, tag, and races. We would play in the dirt and the subject rarely came up. I think it was mostly because they saw a kid like them throwing the ball or grabbing on to them. If there was a 'real negro' in front of them, their behavior could've been different. That was the strange paradox in it all. I didn't have to endure the typical blatant isolation, like the three or four brown skin kids . . . and seeing that, I was not eager to give up my friends and fun.

One day while we were outside, we saw a young black man walking down the road in front of the school. "Is that your brother?" one of the kids asked. "No" I said, "Mrs. Maddox said your brother is that color—Is your brother that color?" said another. I understood what Mrs. Maddox had told them, but I would deflect it with honesty. "My brother's not that color" I said, kind of matter-of-fact. Indeed, none of my brothers were that color, that young man was quite dark-skinned. I was being truthful, if not answering the real question they had. Again, an awkward moment, but not something that would cause them to rethink our friendship, that would happen more often as everyone got older. I would never deny that I was 'colored', but it was not something I would volunteer, sometimes even when the conversation was about whites and blacks. I was afraid, afraid that my friends would not be my friends. As an adult you can say things like . . . "what about dignity" "what, were you ashamed?" easy to say when the confrontation is immediate and direct, but when they have already become friends it's more like the experience of Jews or Gays perhaps, not that you want it kept a secret or feel embarrassed, but you know it can change things. It is probably easier to have it known from the beginning, but you want the chance to be friends first.

I did have a good white friend that year, Barry Poole. Barry and I developed the typical close friendship of two ten-year old boys that loved to laugh and play. Apparently, too much for Mrs. Maddox, she failed us both that year. The only two in the class; the nigger, and the nigger lover, you could say. I don't deny I was a poor student that year but not the worst in the class. My mother was heartbroken that I had to repeat the fifth grade. Still, she didn't prolong any anger or disappointment toward me; she just simply looked me in the face and gave me a lifelong rule. "This is what you get when you don't work and do what you should." That's true, but also true was the degree of Mississippi in Mrs. Maddox.

This was just a year or two after 'Miss Mississippi 1963,' the state queen, and her family were literally run out of the state for simply talking with young white college students that had come down during "Freedom Summer" 1964 to help register blacks to vote. That mentality holds no compunction about failing a little colored child, as white looking as I was, and his delusional friend. Of course at the time I didn't assign it to anything other than what my mother said, and she was right, but today, in hindsight it certainly makes me think. For a hundred years, there had been no policy, no municipal design, no school decisions or road improvements, no healthcare or gas stations, no nothing considered without considering race. The component of race was as relevant as any law of physics. The issue was ever present, with relatives, neighbors, and of course classmates.

Despite the complications of my situation as a child, I remember myself as generally pretty happy. I had good friends and a close family. I had mischievous times and just laid back times. All the kinds of things most kids enjoy I enjoyed. While my skin was white, I had a black body, athletic with strong thighs, competitive in every way with my black friends. We didn't have swimming pools and summer camp or vacations in Europe, but I enjoyed the laughter and fun that is the essence of childhood. I simply had to learn to live with a part of myself that could be uncomfortable, at times painful. It is hard to say if I would be a different person had I not looked so White, while being Black.

Oddly, my looks, while extremely problematic, gave me an advantage that very few blacks or whites experienced in the sixties. In general, even today, the way in which blacks and whites interact is often reserved. As comfortable as each may seem to be, we maintain a buffer, where certain opinions are kept close, for fear of damaging the conversation or relationship, understandably. What might be considered a buffer today was a great chasm in the sixties. If, or when, there was interaction it was simple and basic, if not rude or insulting by one side or the other. I'm speaking about the average encounter. I know there were many enlightened circles that continued the progress of society. However, my circles were like the vast majority. If there was a group of blacks talking and a white approached, there was immediate silence as if to say, "What do you want?" The same for whites, even though the chance a black would approach a white group would be almost out of the question, unless it was 'business.' You might be one person at school or work and another at home or in your community. For that reason, when you encountered the other race they were received with prejudice and suspicion, so both sides were operating in that mode, in a sense, not themselves. We were ourselves when we were with our race, with each other. In that regard, for me, it was a tale of four worlds . . . Black or White in a White world, and Black or White in a Black world, always. I had the opportunity to be with whites, or blacks, when they were not in that mode. I could sit among whites, who thought I was white and witness the humor, kindness, and open friendship that few blacks could experience about them. Likewise, when I was with friends from the neighborhood, or relatives, I saw the genuine black side of things, not the role playing that would be necessary around whites, and certainly not the media stereotype.

Of course, it had the downside at times, hearing the ugly opinions about 'niggers', and being perceived as white from blacks that did not know me. Interestingly, when either side found out, any strong disbelief or incredulous responses were almost exclusively from whites. Black folk could believe there were those like me. Throughout our history the slave was after all a slave, for any purpose, leaving all manner of complexions in that wake, even mine. While characters so light as to confuse white folk popped up in several Faulkner novels, that great southern son so lauded for his grasp of the southern psyche, the reality of those characters seem voluntarily absent in that psyche.

In the sixties, the 'Great Society' was realizing our nation was home of many different needs. We grew up as we saw the country grow; race and class, sexual exploration, drug abuse, and the fact that we were fighting a war, losing young boys who would share foxholes in Asia but could not share fountains at home, strange, but not incongruous at all, a complication that would color, no pun, all life in America. The blend of white, black and Indian would create people and stories greater than fiction. A blond haired hazel-blue eyed black woman . . . exists only in America. It would only be in America because only here can you be defined not by the imperfections of one's will, but by the impurities of one's whiteness.

My aunt, Brunette, was one such woman, a petite beautiful blonde with hazel-blue eyes. My mother's younger sister, she was one of those that could have easily 'passed' in her day. She instead married a handsome brown-skinned man named Harry Taylor. How they moved about in public must have been a constant calculation. One can only imagine some of the things they experienced. The story of life for them in the fifties must have been the stuff of movies, but they went about it, having thirteen children amidst it all. The sixties brought tides of change that chipped away at those social walls, tides that slowly changed how we looked at each other, but not necessarily, how we saw each other. The children of Brunette, and my mother Ruth, would field the question our time demanded . . . "Am I black enough?" By the late sixties black was beautiful, black was power, to be "young, gifted and black was where it's at" went the melody of a popular song. The burgeoning awareness of young blacks that their nappy hair and big lips were just what the "hip" pop culture wanted was all the more difficult for the high yellow, good haired Negroes like us.

For me, it was a regular taunt that I could always expect from friends, family and even those I didn't know well but they knew me, or perhaps about me. It was rarely meant to offend but more as a quick and easy place to have a laugh. I remember my cousins, Brunette's kids, who'd sing a popular jingle when I visited. It was from a fast food hamburger chain called Whiteys . . . "Hey Whitey, I like your clean white towers and your clean white hamburgers too . . ." I never got upset because we always had the most fun together. But that kind of innocent fun was not impotent. I absorbed the wave, however gentle, as I did those that would crash with malice.

In school, I seemed to gravitate to kids who might be avoided by most classmates, for whatever reason. One day, in my 'second' year of fifth grade, we were all out on the playground, in a typical game of dodge ball, two kids, one at each end of the court and all the others in-between. The idea was to dodge the ball as it was thrown from one end to the other. The sound of screams and laughter would almost drown out the loud 'ping' of the big rubber ball used. It was the quintessential image of children at play. I was pretty quick so usually one of the last remaining on the court, jumping over the ball, spinning to avoid it, and taunting the goalie. After the game, we recalled all the close dodging with breathless excitement. I looked over to the side and saw this boy leaning against a light pole. He had his hands in his pockets and seemed to be daydreaming. I wondered why he was not playing. He would shift his weight occasionally as if to relax better, and often blink his eyes, involuntarily, it was obvious he was alone, no apparent friends.

His name was Fabian Rivadeneira; he was a new kid from South America, born in Ecuador. Unfortunately, Fabian contracted Polio after birth, one year before the vaccine reached Ecuador. The disease left him with a deformed leg, much thinner and weaker, and he was unable to run or do most of the physical activities that were constant for other kids. I suppose I felt sorry for him, but it may also have been a degree of empathy. I could feel loneliness in him, and while I was engaged with other kids, I understood it. I approached Fabian and tried to get to know him. He was very shy and didn't talk much at first. I thought Fabian was such a cool name. "It's like a movie star name," I said to him. "What is it?"— "It's Spanish," he said, but would add nothing else. He was very shy and fought to control his nervous blinking. I didn't learn about Ecuador or the polio until later when we became friends. He, like me, did not volunteer information like that until necessary. It was a little longer before he found out I was black. "Really? . . . you can't be . . . wow" was his response, almost like he thought it was cool. He did, however, also find my name curious. Hoover is my first name, and by that virtue, what I was called by my classmates until the end of high school. "Hoooova, that's kinda funny, what is that" he joked. It would be the reason for occasional laughs all through my school years. Most thought I was named for my father, Charles Hoover, and in a way I was, but I am Hoover LaMonte, not a junior. Hundreds of times I've told how my father was born the night Herbert Hoover was elected president and that I was born on Herbert Hoover's birthday. It would never lessen the comic nature kids would find in the name but gave it legitimacy. Fabian and I became good friends from that day on and all through high school, he only started calling me Monte long after those school days. We still remain in touch today, after 50 years, he is my oldest friend.

It was another world at home and in my neighborhood, where virtually all my friends attended a different school. Providence Park had a playground that was the focal point for all the kids. It had a basketball court, a few sets of swings, sand boxes, large areas to run or play kickball, and a small building for bathrooms and to hold the balls of various games. Pool, or billiards, was popular. There was no pool table, of course, but we had a small table version that would rest on the top of a trashcan. It was used for several games; we used the same pieces used for checkers as our pool balls. They would slide into net pockets that hung at the corners. The playground was one of the first places you learned to talk "smack," the jargon of confidence and ridicule of your opponent. There was something about the innocent witty attacks on each other, which not only heightened the value of the contest but our relationships as well. It let us realize, as the old saying goes, it's not if you win or lose, because the fun was in both. It seemed everyone had a nickname too; just as common as the Ronalds and Michaels were those called Fish or Booky, or Red Duck, or Bugg. How they got the name was usually evident after meeting or knowing that person. I, actually didn't have one, my first name was funny enough "Hoova," when I wasn't Monte or sometimes "Red."

"I'm going there to fight for you, Red" a muscular, dark-skinned young man said to me. Howard Braxton lived directly across the street from the playground. Howard was there one evening like many from the neighborhood, playing ball or just hangin' out. The park in Providence Park was about a half square block large and it was the gathering point of a whole range of kids from four to twenty four, it was the eye of the neighborhood. We were standing around with some of the older guys and they were talking about the Army and the draft and a place on the other side of the world, Vietnam. Howard was in the Army, leaving soon for that Vietnam. He had a somewhat resigned mood about it, but he played it off like brothers do, while the others talked shit about how he was a bad mutha and he'd be Ok.

We all knew about that war, and yet, it didn't really touch me until that evening when Howard looked down at me and said he would fight for me. It was easy to see he was bothered, but I also felt he was absolutely sincere. I didn't have anything I could say, I just looked at him and felt a sad mixture of admiration and sorrow. I had a feeling though, a strong sense that he really cared about me in a noble kind of way. Howard knew he might not return, and I felt if he didn't, it would be because he fought for me. He fought for the weird little light skin kid in his hood, our hood. "Red," had value to him. When Howard Braxton said he would essentially die for me, I felt unconditionally accepted by that brother. I was learning being black was not so much an issue of biology or blood, but more a distinct African American experience, at once narrow and broad. Sadly, I don't remember if Howard made it back OK. I'm pretty sure he did, but I'm not certain for some reason. I just recall that time at the playground and the clear impression it made on me. "Red" was getting a little bit blacker.

My older siblings at Henrico High would stand out beyond the legacy of integration. My brother, Butch, would be the first black on the football team, famous to some yet infamous to others. My brother Chuck, would be a star athlete racing in cross country distance running, not exactly the event 'brothers' were known for then. He would be the "fly in the soup" at most track meets but proved without doubt he belonged. And Chuck, or Henry, as he was known, would leave an indelible mark, literally. He sculpted a large Warrior bust that would stand as our school mascot for decades. The "Indian Head," or "Warrior" was the senior class gift. The sculpture bore his hand scribbled signature in the base. It stood about 3 feet high, sculpted from clay and cast in bronze, resting atop a five foot pedestal. It was another irony; a white school with an Indian mascot created by one of its first black students. Chuck even made the local paper with his picture at work on the three-foot bust. 'The Warrior' sat at the main entrance to the school, commanding the attention of any visitor. It was where we assembled for everything from pep rallies to student demonstrations.

I remember a small demonstration there my sophomore year. About 20 students stood and spoke in support of more African American studies and recognition of Black history. A young girl, feeling the spirit of the Black Panther movement, went on about the "color of America." "It's a white world! And we don't have any place here!" The red, black and green dashiki she wore serving as uniform for the message, not the weather of February. I was huddling with others in the group but was soon singled out by the young Angela Davis wannabe. Shaking her large Afro with indignant flare, she looked at me and said, "The colors of this country are just like him . . . red hair, white skin and blue eyes." Virtually everyone in the crowd knew I was black, not to mention my eyes were brown, but she obviously enjoyed the laughter at my expense, glaring at me as if I was some stupid white boy trying to be righteous. I was, as Malcolm X put it, the blue-eyed devil. I looked at the strong proud face of that Indian head and felt embarrassed, and angered, because she knew the history of black folk, just not the history of blacks at Henrico High. She simply had an agenda to rant against "whitey." She didn't know a black kid had made the Indian head at her back, much less my brother, and didn't know that the very first "Miss Warrior" was black, my sister. Funny, the chances are the judges of that Miss Warrior pageant were oblivious as well. My sister, Valerie, would win the very first Miss Warrior pageant in 1967. Valerie sang and danced to win that title to the shock of her fellow contestants, who had by their own hand already voted her "Miss Congeniality." The visiting judges likely did not realize Valerie was black, or surely would not have given the award to the most deserving. While the young sister at the rally went on about unrecognized contributions, the ignorance was ironic.

The year 1967 was a difficult but remarkable senior year for Valerie, culminating with that win of the first Miss Warrior. Singing and dancing a performance of "The Shadow of your Smile" from the movie "The Sandpiper," the song had very poignant meaning for her.

Theodore Hundley was a tall, dark and handsome man. He lived a few miles from us in the Barton Heights neighborhood. Theodore was an athletic and confident young man with a smooth voice and dimpled smile. He met Valerie through my older brother Butch. He was soon her boyfriend and would come to "court" her as they used to say. "I'm gonna build you a peanut butter factory" he once told me as I ate multiple sandwiches while he sat with Valerie on our living room couch. The factory would have to wait for some time though, Theodore was joining the Marines. It would be hard to picture a more attractive set of 'Dress Blues' when Theodore filled them. But there was a problem . . . it was 1965. Vietnam was a spot where advisors and action was gearing up. Troops were going but it was not at the level it would be. Theodore was sent for a short time to the Dominican Republic, but was soon off to serve his year in 'Nam, an all but oblivious place to kids like me. He did his year and while there purchased an engagement ring in Saigon, hoping to surprise Valerie when he returned home. He waited till the last week to purchase it, a short one week left for him to keep the ring safe.

That week, the second week of November 1966, was a time most fifth graders, including me, spent evenings watching TV. On Monday night, November 7, I was watching the movie 'Hans Christian Anderson' starring Danny Kaye. His big and bright red hair was just another shade of gray on our TV. During the show our phone rang, with the clanging sound of metal on metal, and was quickly answered by me. On the other end was a familiar voice . . . Theodore's mother. "Hi sweetheart, this is Mrs. Hundley, is your mother there?" The tone of her voice was very distressed, as if she was in pain; it had the unmistakable tremble that accompanies tears. As I gave the phone to my mother I followed it to her ear and watched as her face became bent and wrinkled. "Oh Elsie, oh Lord . . . Lord have mercy . . . please Jesus" she softly cried. My mother shuttered, as if cold, as she sat at our kitchen table and wiped away tears. My little sister Vicki slowly walked into the kitchen and sat on my mother's lap looking sadly at her. Mrs. Hundley had lost her son Theodore. Killed one week before he was due home, one week was all he had left, one week. To lose a child that way, so close to being safe, must make one curse the very concept of life if it can bring a pain like this. My mother wiped her tears but more would flow. I was pretty much stunned. It was only the second death I had experienced, the first of my grandfather two years earlier. Valerie was not home, she worked evenings at the phone company and got home around 9pm. My mother agonized the moments waiting.

When Valerie walked in she instantly knew something was wrong. Before the door closed, before my mom could hardly speak, Valerie was dropping to the floor. "God no! No, you are wrong! God you are wrong!" she moaned. For a few seconds, we stood silently looking as she laid crying and writhing at the foot of the door. Her fist hit the floor softly in a slow-motion fight, without hope. Valerie fought to tell us how she had dropped his picture from her purse while riding home on the bus, and how she didn't pick it up for a while. "I didn't get it, it fell and I didn't get it," she whispered to the floor. Devastated, anguished and perhaps shamed, she seemed to believe that that moment of neglect was why, why God had done her wrong. We all stood in our place, motionless, looking down at her, lost. I questioned God too, as absolute as my mother had raised us in this belief, even a ten year old could see the outrageous tragedy which to me was like a sin committed by God. Why must we sometimes suffer so profoundly from the random and delicate course of life? If not random, is it Him? Fifty years later the question remains, only consoled by a law of nature, but that all life must follow. Things like this are "meant to be" mama would say, "the Lord works in mysterious ways." Those words might serve as an answer but little solution to the trauma.

Valerie stayed on the floor for what seemed like a long time until the tears dried. Later that night, Theodore's younger brother, Melvin, came by. He didn't seem to hold the pain the rest of us did. Perhaps it was the way he handled things as a seventeen-year-old boy. Perhaps, it was just the way a ten-year-old perceived it. We didn't say very much for a long time; my mother's absolute faith in Jesus was all she could give her child or herself.

When the holidays came that December, we spent time at Mrs. Hundley's home, my parents offering what comfort they could as she lay in her bed, accepting a pain that does not end. Christmas 1966 is a timeless moment in my memory, full of soft colors glowing in the Hundley home. It was there I watched 'color' TV for the first time. "In living color" the announcer said, as the NBC peacock opened a rainbow of feathers. That new television, likely acquired with the money received from Theodore's death benefit, served as a distraction in their home with all the other colorful lights of the season. Yet, serving only to belie the state of a stricken family . . . a family and a young woman, left with just the shadow of a smile.

Carrot top, 1959.
I actually remember that moment.

"Integrating" elementary school, 1963.

My paternal grandparents,
Amanda Greene and Charlie Richardson.

At the old home in Bracey, Virignia.
My mother, Ruth, center, and me to her left acting silly crossing my eyes,
with relatives around my great grandmother.

Shared feelings, a boy and his dog.

Showdown, 1965, my mom and little sister Vicki with my big brother,
Chuck, at our home in Providence Park.

My amazing, dedicated parents, Ruth and Hoover, in the late sixties.

Just another fifteen-year-old in Richmond, Virginia, 1971.

My best friend in the late sixties was actually someone I'd see only a few weeks a year. He was a kid who had come to visit his aunt for a couple weeks one summer, and we were fast friends from the start. Richard Pearson was the nephew of our neighbor Mrs. Braxton, the mother of Howard, the soldier from a few years earlier. Mrs. Braxton lost her cat one day, and I was able to catch it and bring it to her. That's when I met Richard. He lived in Boston, but his parents were separated, and he had come for a summer visit. He came each of the next 3 summers for about a month and he was the closest thing to a "best friend at camp" I would have. We would spend all day together, working on model cars, listening to music, playing with his cassette recorder, making grill cheese sandwiches, or just talking and laughing. Man, did we laugh a lot. Richard was light-skinned as well, but only so that he looked Mexican or Puerto Rican, with very black hair, 'good hair'. He had a typical Boston accent, where people drove 'cahrs' and drank 'tonic' instead of sodas. My good memories of summer's long days and evenings were spent hanging out with Richard, hanging out with the music of the wild late sixties.

The summer of 1969 was one of those summers, but it was filled with other memories. It was the summer I spent two weeks on Long Island, NY with my grandparents. They lived way out on the island where there were many potato farms and duck farms, a smell that was unmistakable. We would drive to visit them every summer, and it was always easy to know when you could stop asking, "Are we there yet?" They also had their own garden with fresh vegetables that I've always used as a reference for the way a cucumber or tomato should taste. My parents thought I could be a help for them if I stayed this time. My dad's sister lived right next door with her family so I was able to spend time bonding with my cousins, Gregory and Wendy. They were a few years older than I, so it wasn't a lot of playing, just the neat stuff you're anxious to do like a "teenager." Grandpa Harris, as we called him, was not my biological grandfather, he married my dad's mother in 1946. My father's real dad, Charlie Richardson, died in 1940 from pneumonia or "the grip" as they called it. Walter Harris and my grandma moved to Long Island, NY. I never knew why there, but they took my dad's younger sister, Ruth, with them. Riverhead was the closest thing to a city near them. It was a small town with a few banks and supermarkets, a central intersection that you call "downtown", and a movie theater.

That summer, 'McKenna's Gold' was playing there, a western starring Gregory Peck. I remember it fondly; the only time I ever went to the movies with my dad. He was a fan of Gregory Peck, who played the tall, quiet, diligent and fair characters my dad enjoyed, most famously as Atticus Finch in "To Kill a Mockingbird." The dark, cool theater was cozy, and I felt a closeness to my father that was special. That day, we were buddies seeing a movie together. It was not that we didn't spend time together, we did, but most of it was in the context of work in the yard or with him on some task. I'll always remember one time when I went to the grocery store with him. He had his paycheck and he showed me the grand amount—one hundred eighty-two dollars. He grinned with such pride at that amount. The total grocery bill that day was twenty-seven dollars, including Cheerios and a half gallon of ice cream . . . celebration!

But, the candy bar, the movie, the grins, were not a celebration but a confirmation. "Can you imagine all that gold? You wouldn't know what to do with it, huh?" he whispered during one scene, challenging the notion that so much wealth was necessary. He had a point, because that afternoon with my dad is an absolute treasure.

That summer was also when the "Eagle" landed on the moon. I watched it with my grandparents at two in the morning on their flickering black and white TV. It was somewhat surreal to be in their small dark home with just the light from the moon, so to speak. The blurry image of Neil Armstrong was not convincing to my grandfather, "He ain't on no moon, nah I don't believe it . . . he probably somewhere in Arizona or something," he protested. At eighty, Grandpa Harris was incredulous, he had seen all the amazing advances of the twentieth century: cars, planes, radio, TV, etc. But, a leap for mankind, that could rival the wheel itself? I think he just didn't believe he could be lucky enough to witness that. Grandma was less skeptical, "I don't know, maybe they could be up there" she said in a half sleep state, probably not caring much one way or the other. Amanda, my dad's mom, was about seventy-four with very strong opinions about everything and would share them. She had been an attractive woman, with a blend of American Indian and Black, and who knows. Grandma Harris, as we knew her, had lost her husband, my dad's dad, leaving her with six children. Grandma, like virtually all black grandmas, was always happy to fix food, food that was good but would often bring with it a piece of her long hair. "Durn, grandma, we got hair in the eggs again" my older brother Butch once laughed, as my other siblings laughed even harder. "Be quiet boy, ain't nothing wrong with them eggs, I ain't studdin bout no hair" she snapped back, holding back her own grin. She had thick wavy black hair with a strong jaw and forehead that could release into a proud smile.

That grin was beaming one day when she and I went to the market together. Grandma walked through that market like she owned it. Sure, she probably knew everyone that worked there; still, she seemed to speak to every soul in the store. I mostly looked down at the floor or at her opaque light brown nylon hosiery that went up from her heavy healed black shoes and curled down above the knee, just covered by her dress. As we stood in the checkout the clerk looked at me while she opened her small purse that held her money. "That's my grandson," she proclaimed with such pride and intent that I was naturally embarrassed. She grinned at the clerk as if to say "See, I have white in my family, isn't that nice?" The clerk smiled, amused but not moved; he seemed to just want to get on with the groceries and go home, just like I did. Grandma looked down at me and smiled as if I had done something to make her proud. I started to rock on my sneakers and play with the moving belt that glided the groceries to the register. I was happy my grandmother was happy with me, rare and precious in her mind as any child is to their grandparent. However, at this moment it was not so much family as it was social. I had been able to elevate her place in society. After seventy-five years, at that moment, she felt a bit more "acceptable." That mentality of grandma was always, 'if it's white it's right'. I can't explain that, other than perhaps a result of messages, layered like an onion, on the lives of millions. Layered messages composing our nation's bedrock question: Race.

When my grandmother moved to Long Island in 1946, I'm not sure if it was for any reason other than why others were going north, to find work that allowed some degree of dignity and security, to escape the glaring yoke of Jim Crow. Perhaps the North was not so much better than the South, but at least it was not as officially decreed. The South, as MLK said, "played their role to the hilt." I can understand the role my grandmother played, after all. Her experiences were shaped in a time when lynchings were as common as a summer thunderstorm. She had known of more than a few by her twenties, and there must have been a very clear pragmatism in her approach to white people, and now, the strategic success of having a "white" grandchild. I didn't know grandma too well, seeing her only once or twice a year. She died in 1970, but I have to believe she held a layer of deep militancy and revolt somewhere under that veil of, as perceived by many whites, a soft sycophant colored woman.

Meanwhile, lots of brothers were getting drafted in the late sixties, my oldest brother Charles, or "Butch" as we called him, had joined the Navy in 1964 and spent time in the Mediterranean, but the draft caught Chuck. The same summer I was being doted over, he was in Vietnam. He was selected in December '68 while in college at Virginia Union University; but the luck got even better, he was in the Marines. We went to his boot camp graduation in Paris Island, S.C that winter. It was exciting for me to see the base and all the military vehicles and soldiers. The graduation day was bright and cold, and it seemed difficult for the Marines to stand at attention in the blustery wind. I remember the moment they were released, as they threw their caps to the sky, hugged, and shook hands. There were families that cried; I thought at the time from pride. Chuck was smiling as most of the Marines were, but it must have been forced, or certainly stressed. Everyone knew it would be just a few short weeks before they headed to 'Nam. 1969 was the year when the war was on everybody's mind, every day. Years of growing protest, draft-dodgers, TV images and the weekly "dead" count, was not lost on my parents. We toured the base and saw things like tanks on display and the barracks, as well as the small theater they had. We were guided in to see a short film on the heroics of the Marine Corps, and the legendary scenes of Iwo Jima, not Vietnam.

It was a warmer day in Richmond when Chuck left. He had his duffle bag full and hugged us while we stood in our driveway. My dad, who was not a big talker anyway, was unusually quiet and stoic. They didn't linger much and got in the car. It was a very sad moment watching the car pulling away going up Richmond Henrico Turnpike. From behind, Chuck looked like a little boy in the seat beside my dad, maybe he was slumped, but they looked like a dad with his young son going for a ride, a very difficult ride.

I would spend other days that summer and fall sitting in Chuck's car in the backyard, listening to the radio or reading the Marine's 'Leatherneck' magazine we'd receive. The big white 1960 Impala was a kind of hideout for me, where I could imagine conversations and adventures as I listened to songs like the Temptations' "Ball of Confusion." It was a big hit that year. It hit the mark about society then and now. It was that fall I started at Henrico High school, which included grades seven through twelve. With close to two thousand students, I was pretty excited.

"Yasser Arafat is the leader of the PLO. Can anyone tell me what that stands for?" my seventh grade history teacher asked. Like typical young teenagers, the response was mostly sarcastic, poking fun at the picture of Arafat with his headdress and large nose. I sat in the middle of class behind Chris Roberts, a small frame kid with blond hair who liked to speak up, even when he was only guessing. "Is it the Palestine army name?" he offered while jutting his hand up high. "No, but very close," the teacher replied. She went on about all the various players in the region and the on-going conflict with Israel, and the wars since 1948. She talked about the swing of the pendulum as an example of how things must go sometimes to change, that sometimes there must be over correction, as things reach center. The subject naturally found its way to our clashes at home over race, and of course Vietnam, and all the boys from Richmond in the war. Chris again raised his hand . . . "Did you know the guy that made the Indian head (the mascot sculpture in front of the school) is in Vietnam?"— "Yes, I know," she said. "They said he has malaria,"— "Oh really?"— "Yeah, and I heard they don't expect him to make it," Chris said as he wiggled in front of me with the giddy arrogance of a teacher's pet. I winced and felt confused. I knew Chris didn't know what the fuck he was talking about, but hearing it made it somehow real. "My . . . I didn't know that," Mrs. Grey said with a low voice. It took me off guard a bit, I knew Chuck had malaria and was on a hospital ship, but I had not heard that! I started to slowly slump in my chair expecting reaction. Some of the other kids in the class whispered, "That's Hoover's brother, yeah, it is, it's his brother." Mrs. Grey looked at me with a sad questioning look, and I dropped my head. My brother would be fine, but at that moment, feeling the energy of the whole class, it seemed like he really was going to die. I felt a heaviness as if it was true, tears came and I could feel and hear the sighs from some of the girls who also got emotional. Mrs. Grey offered a soft assurance and gently changed the subject. The rest of the day was a mixture of embarrassment and well wishes, and of course, the usual, "I didn't know he was colored . . ."

Years later Chuck told me how he did almost die from it. He was fighting in one of the hottest spots of the war, around DaNang in 1970 as an M60 machine gunner. The jungle served as an enemy itself inflicting monsoons and disease. Chuck became ill but could not convince the medics it was serious. It was not unheard of for soldiers to feign illness or injury, or actually inflict a shot intentionally to get out of "the bush." With fever and fatigue overwhelming him, he desperately needed attention. One morning while using the bathroom, that being the jungle, his eyes fell on the pocket of his knapsack and a bottle of hot sauce. Many marines used it to flavor their bland ready to eat meals. With barely a thought, instinctively he grabbed it. That hot sauce appeared like the ubiquitous blood of that war and could also appear in his shit. So it did. Chuck knew that internal bleeding would be something they took serious, spitting up blood or . . . blood in the feces. The medics did test, finding malaria. He was pulled out of combat and sent for treatment. That probably saved his life, not only because the malaria was treated, but also because soon after he left his platoon the machine gunner, who had replaced him, was killed. Chuck was never really proud of that story, given the sacrifice he had witnessed, and the fate of his replacement. But to me, it is almost Shakespearean, the kind of story my classmate, and class pet, Chris, would have relished. There were not many stories from Chuck about Vietnam when he returned, mostly about characters that were fellow marines and life in the jungle, from snakes to rock throwing apes. The deaths of friends and close calls for himself remained untold for a long time.

Over forty years later my brother would release some of those memories, some of those emotions. He told me of the time he believed the chopper he was in was going down from fire, how at that moment he believed he would die, and his thoughts were of my mother and how she would suffer. He told me of the many firefights he was in, the penetrating monsoon and the difficult witness to suffering civilians. The Vietnam War was particularly devastating to millions of village people across the country. Whether from U.S airpower or Viet Cong retaliation, there are estimates of over a million civilian deaths between 1965-1974. Today, the sad truth is the same; we see it in Aleppo, Syria. Still, there are heroes. There are heroes in every war, men and women who do not necessarily display the effectiveness of their training or commitment to their fellow soldiers, but a fulfillment of their love of humanity. My brother received two purple hearts and a cross of gallantry medal for fighting in Vietnam, but no awards for the battle that is in all wars, the battle within.

A normal part of that war was to clear villages of the enemy, who were rarely evident until they struck, sometimes even children themselves. The crazy nightmare of not knowing who the enemy might be, and the resulting rage, could sometimes lead to whole massacres like that at My Lai in 1968. Chuck told me of the time they entered a village and began the 'sweep' to find any weapons or indication of Viet Cong. Some of the Marines were eager to find revenge for the recent loss of buddies and hoped for a reason to kill something that was Vietnamese. At one point, a small group seized a shivering young girl, perhaps thirteen, in front of crying older women. The intent was clear; they felt justified, that all is fair in war. Chuck said he felt something so fundamentally moving he stepped in and confronted them. "Marines don't rape little girls," he shouted as another marine joined Chuck's side. There was yelling and cursing to the point Chuck said the hands and arms of everyone tensed around their weapons. One of them came at Chuck and stumbled over a large pot of rice, and they both fell to ground. The villagers, mostly older men and women huddled in squatting groups, cried and protested in a language nobody understood, and everyone struggled to understand the madness around them. Fortunately, at that moment a lieutenant came up the path and yelled everyone to attention. The young girl was grabbed by her grandmother and they quickly moved away. As they did, the grandmother looked at Chuck, and with their eyes, they both expressed an appreciation for how, at least in that moment of the war, someone was saved. That old woman and young girl were thankful to the real Marine.

Holding on to your conscience must be one of the toughest things in war. My brother Chuck is a war hero, not just because of his actions to serve his fellow Americans but because of his ability to save his humanity in the belly of war.

Five

By the seventies, many white kids were seeing things with a fresh perspective, like every new generation, but now able to judge blacks personally, not continuing the handed down bigotry of many parents. Bigotry, even subtle and not classic "Jim Crow," was institutional. I remember my high school yearbook and all the pictures of staff and faculty. The captions would read 'Mr. Paul Jones teaches science, or Mrs. Beverly Smith is our Librarian,' etc. There was a picture of our head custodian sitting on the bike he used to get around our open campus. Underneath it read, "Leroy does his daily duties on his Spaceflyer." "Leroy" was easily in his mid-fifties but didn't rank a last name, or even a "Mr. Leroy." The damn bike had equal billing, still 3/5 of a man. However, just the acknowledgement of his work was progress I suppose.

The influence of home and old perspectives remained strong for one of my white friends, Bill McLaughlin. Bill was from Savannah, Georgia. We became friends in the fifth or sixth grade when they moved to Richmond. He would brag about Georgia and a grand new amusement park that opened the year they left, "Six Flags Over Georgia." "It's better than Disneyland" he boasted. We often shared laughs about the TV shows "Gomer Pyle" and "Get Smart." By the seventh grade, however, Bill became totally aloof, not speaking at all and finding reasons to avoid me. It was a glaring avoidance. I had an idea what it was, and it didn't really bother me. By now, I knew that race was a factor, a law of nature. Like Bill, I too, was finding that in middle school you begin to learn about each other in a different context. That one's race or religion, oddly enough, could change who you were. When we were kids things were on a very core level, did you like this toy or that game, was your sense of humor the same, did you like the same foods, music, sports? But later, we learn that things about your friend's family could mean you shouldn't like them. Bill and I became friends as kids, but as he learned about my family, his family made it clear, "we don't associate with niggers, no matter how white they look." That's not a quote, but I'm sure it must have gone something like that. Bill had much pride in Georgia, so I can imagine the great "Gone with the Wind" history his folks told.

One cool fall morning I saw Bill walking with a girl, they seemed to lean on each other for warmth going through the open campus. Like any thirteen-year-old, I joked about it, "alright Bill . . . go 'head now," I said, standing with white friends. Bill broke from his companion and walked toward me as if marching, hands straight at his side, back stiff, with a defiant look. When he got to me, without saying a word or showing expression, he took a swing at me. I deflected his arm and from reflex, struck him in the chest. I jumped back and squared up, swinging my arms like a boxer. He stood there for a second with the same unchanged look, perhaps thinking twice about a fight. He walked away without saying a word as a few kids whooped up the moment. I think I know why Bill did it, not because I embarrassed him, not because he wanted to, but because he felt he had to. His family and friends had made him feel stupid to trust his own judgment. He had enjoyed my company, and I had his, but that was not the point. Bill had been betrayed, and in his mind, defeated. He knew he was not to associate with coloreds, much less befriend one, but as a child he was judging me with a clean slate, unaware as most, of the transparent marks against me. Now, his culture and family made him punish himself, unfairly. I suppose he figured I was as guilty as he was, after all, I knew he was white. Was he that mad? Maybe so, but it's not easy for a young teen to attack a good friend. He probably just thought it was easier to hit me, and feel redeemed, than challenge his culture. Like Mrs. Maddox in the fifth grade, he showed how deep the vein of southern pride ran, a vein that could somehow bypass the heart. We never talked again, and I never saw him with that girl again, to her credit.

"Black Power" was giving kids my age a fresh image of themselves, and that made my looks/image even more difficult. I didn't have a big problem making friends, or having as much fun as any kid, it was just that rarely a day passed that I didn't have to confront some degree of offensive speculation from others. It was tiring and frustrating. There were days when I would sit alone on our front steps and sense myself separate from my body, a meditation or astral projection, feeling I was actually floating, looking down at myself from above. I would think about growing up and being just a face in the crowd, the kind of bobbing head in those compressed shots of city life on TV, anonymous and unnoticed. I suppose my brothers and sisters felt the same to some extent, but having such white skin and red hair and being a boy, it was different for me. Today, I sometimes think it left me without strong ambition, or a drive for success, as success can bring attention. I guess that excuse is as good as any.

———

"Here . . ." my brother Chuck motioned with his mouth closed and chest tight, he extended his arm toward me and jabbed it a couple times. I was about seventeen and would hang out with him and his friends occasionally. Chuck had been home from Vietnam a year or so and we'd listen to music or talk trash. Talking 'trash' was a given no matter what the reason we got together, and Chuck was a master. That day at his friend's apartment there would be long pauses between the laughs and banter, as everyone would contemplate things like the Aloe plant or a glass bowl on the table. Chuck slowly released the pressure in his chest, looking at me with disappointment, and a thick creamy smoke cloaked the amused gaze of his buddies. "Here man, it's cool . . . jive turkey," he said. I did ultimately smoke reefer that day, if only to show my brother I trusted him. The early seventies was full of skepticisms about anything you had been told by "The Man," whether it was about race or law or history or even what was good or bad for your health. Young people were already rejecting many social ideas on how to look and how to live, and it was reasonable to wonder why marijuana was illegal, since alcohol and cigarettes killed thousands every year. I did not feel the herb at first; it was, to me, a non-event. Trying to feel older and impressive, I explained to the brothers that it was mental, that you think you are "high" and therefore you are. A knowing laughter burst from each of them as they looked at me, and back at each other, only to crack up further from some unspoken message between them. The broad grins and glassy eyes relaxed as they debated the value of my impression. "Yo, Chuck, that's deep though man . . . cause knowledge is power, and a thought or belief is like knowledge, you dig?" "Yeeaaah . . . you right, we'll see if he just thinks he's hungry in a half hour," Chuck replied. The laughter erupted again and led to coughing and watery eyes. The coughing and laughter, the red eyes, and "munchies" would find me often in a few years, a habit that remained through my twenties.

Volumes have been written on the terrible impact of drugs and alcohol on countless Americans and particularly Black Americans, my brother among them. Chuck had also started using heroin in Vietnam, a remedy found by thousands of soldiers to combat the fear. He concealed it for twenty years while reaching, then losing, great notoriety. It is a long and fascinating book in itself and I hope he writes it. Someone should. In the seventies, in my environment, it was rare to meet someone who "would never" or "had never" smoked pot. The notion that marijuana was dangerous or unhealthier than Marlboros, was generally rejected. Cocaine, however, was seen as dangerously addictive, and I, personally, knew of hardly anyone that did it. The reefer experience with my brother was one of only a couple times in high school. I was an athlete and my circle was not inclined as some. That would change in college, but it was rare until then. There were some who got involved deeply, their lessons more about law and order as risk. One high school classmate, Dewitt, was a very easygoing and mild-mannered teen. He probably smoked a lot more than we thought because he would eventually sell to people. That was not smart; we knew the business of pot was a lot more risky than the buzz of pot. One night, Dewitt was found beaten to death on a street not far from his home. He was eighteen. They assumed it was a robbery or something gone bad with a deal. I never learned the real story. It was a rare case, but it would portend the violence of the eighties, as cocaine became the octane for so much tragedy.

High school introduced me to team sports, football and track, all four years. We won regional titles in both, and our track team remained undefeated in dual meets for three consecutive years. There are lots of memories of pleasant spring afternoons running long miles with my teammates. Track was not intense like football, where you had a coach yelling at you and at your side most of the time. We usually had sets of stretches and routines that were left to us, that allowed a jovial bonding between us. I was a good athlete and stood out within the school but was not a standout in the greater region. I did manage to make it to the State track meets each year as a jumper and relay member. The State Championships were pretty exciting, lots of officials and coaches, ribbons and trophies, and of course, girls.

One year I competed in the triple jump and placed sixth, not bad but no ribbon. The first five spots received medals or ribbons, which left me with just the memory, no tangibles. After the event was over I walked away slowly with my head down sighing in disappointment. A white coach, I did not know, walked along with a supportive smile and put his arm over my shoulder as he said, "You did alright, you did alright. You know what your problem is, don't you?" I shook my head thinking I was not hitting my mark or using my arms effectively. "You're the wrong color" he advised with a friendly chuckle. That coach meant no offense, he was simply trying to assure me that those five colored boys could not be out jumped, but I was the best white kid out there. He walked away with a smile and another pat on the back, while I thought to myself, the jokes on you, coach, I'm the wrong color, perhaps, but you've got it right, no white kid can out jump us.

George Wythe was a black school that had a football team that was seen as unbeatable, with linemen the size you see in college. My senior year we had a team that would rival them. We ran a wish-bone offense, and it was seen as the game of the year when we met, the two best teams in the city. I had played wide-receiver my junior year but my senior year was moved to halfback. The game had lots of hype as it was one of the last and would determine the regional champs. That week I developed a high fever and a very bad sore throat that would ultimately require removal of my tonsils. My mother didn't want me to play on the day of the game but knew I would. Game day in high school meant pep rallies and banners, cheerleaders and fight songs. It was unfortunate I could not enjoy it fully; my temperature was over 101 degrees. The evening was not much better but the excitement of the crowd and band gave everyone a boost. The Wythe players were indeed big and strong, but not quick enough for us. It turned out to be my best game with over 100 yards rushing, two touchdowns, and an interception from my safety position. The next day, the sports section of the paper had a large picture of me getting pass the "elite" defenders. It was a great thrill. Lots of players made the paper over the season, but it was my picture that made it in the game of the year. It was the closest I ever got to any celebrated attention. But, I would not receive any offers to play college-level because of my poor grades. There were schools that wanted me to play for them but would not offer scholarships. Again, lesson learned the hard way. Just like the fifth grade, not doing what I should have, to be what I could have.

I was nowhere near the star that Ben Turner was at Henrico. Ben was a neighbor; he and his brothers and sisters lived close and we knew the family well. His older brother, Chris, had actually been the star quarterback for Henrico, in fact, Chris was one of, if not the first, black starting quarterback at a white high school in Virginia. Chris, or "Putt" as we called him, became a close friend after I graduated. We loved to play chess and banter about issues. All the Turner kids were smart, and Ben was no different. He was a couple years ahead of me but we talked a lot at school and he was one of those brothers that was very aware of politics and the evolution of race in America. I remember fondly the way he would spend some lunch breaks with me, a lowly freshman, and talk about politics and society. Outside my brothers and family, it was where I first talked about the issues of our society and the why and how I had to navigate the consequences of my color situation. Ben was definitely the greatest runner of his time, certainly in the Richmond area. There were games when he would average ten yards a carry. He was not a very big player, but his speed, strength, and agility became legendary. The only problem was the way he carried his politics. Ben was outspoken and active with things around campus. That didn't sit too well with the administration. He pushed for Black studies and recognition of the racist conditions in society. I remember a picture of him putting up a poster in school; it was an illustration of a strong muscular black man emerging from the shell of a weak grinning "Stepin Fetchit" type Negro. Ben was standing next to it with a raised "Black Power" fist. It read "Inside every Negro there is a potential Black man!" That kind of thing intimidated many of the white students, and had a labeling affect on him, even though Ben was about the nicest guy you could meet, with a strong sense of humor.

It was expected Ben would receive scholarship offers from around the country, his grades were up to it, but it wasn't the case. For Ben, many big schools did not want an athlete that, through their stardom, expressed opinions that could be "disruptive." That kind of thing was a tightrope many black athletes had to walk in the seventies if they wanted to play for any of the big schools. I'm not sure why he didn't play for an HBCU, although in those days it was very rare that HBCUs would recruit from white schools, I don't really know. He would eventually go to a university out in New Mexico, where again, his confident outspoken position on things was a problem. Ben would not finish college. He ultimately fell into drug use which may have contributed to his premature death from a congenital heart defect. So sad that the passion he had to expose the potential of young black men would be part of the reason he would not fulfill his own; it was sad.

Whether it was the intense frustration of dealing with an overtly racist boss, or as with my brother trying to make it in Vietnam, or the simple curious bravado of youth, the impact of drugs on Black America has been insidious. As a journalist, twenty-five years later, I would see the devastation in housing projects full of thirty-five-year-old grandmothers. Kids of kids, on the street, neglected for the chase of a high and a lover. Young people full of potential but collared by a chain of nihilism and contempt. A long way from the kids I knew at Henrico . . . a long way from being a kid.

Typically, the black students at Henrico were not in drama or band, or science clubs etc., given the handful of blacks at Henrico. The stigma of "trying to be white" kept so many talented young people from the arts and academic excellence. It may be my bad recollection or just the school I attended, but it's how I remember the attitudes of many then. Even in all black schools, it was somehow seen as white-like to be "too" smart. That was one of the ironic consequences of integration in the seventies, creating for some an unfortunate reluctance to be overly smart academically.

There were almost four-hundred graduates from Henrico in June 1975; it was a warm and humid evening on the football field where we sat waiting to be called. I believe my mother and little sister were there but no other family. My mortarboard cap sat precariously on my "wild" hair while I waited for the 'R's. After the ceremony I had no plans, many of us just hung around the parking lot wondering what to do. There was a girl I knew from one of my classes that I started talking to, I didn't know her all that well, but we talked sometimes in class. I felt like the boy in the bubble when it came to girls, not that I wasn't funny and entertaining, or overly shy, but girls were afraid to be seen "in the bubble" so to speak. She was driving her dad's 1973 Chevy "El Camino," it was one of those half-truck half-car models around in the late sixties-early seventies. She was tall and slim with dark blond hair, not a beauty queen but attractive. We talked a bit about graduation and college and she asked me about the race thing, what it was like for me, what I thought about it, etc. She seemed to be fascinated about it, and we ended up riding around and eventually parking. We sat and talked for a while, and she began to act as if she felt affection for me. She stopped talking and just looked at me as she leaned back against the door. We had sex right there in the front seat of that El Camino. We were both on the tall side so trying to do it in the cramped space with a steering wheel was an issue, but the excitement rendered space no problem. It was the last thing I thought would happen to me that night, with no girl friend, no parties, and no plans at all; it was like a surprise graduation gift, crude as it might sound. We barely knew each other and I didn't see her much again after that, what amounted to a one-night stand. The very thing that had been the bane of my youth, this color thing, had maybe served me, again not to sound crude. It seemed to be an emotional thing for her, maybe sympathy or admiration, or maybe and likely just teenage hormones, who knows.

I made several good friends in high school. Derrick Glasper, a teammate who went on to UVA and played pro ball a couple years with the Steelers. William Battle, who joined the Army and spent twenty years there, and "Buck" Gibbs, who has had several careers over the last forty years. Buck and I remain close today, we can't count the times we've hung out and enjoyed laughs while I lived in Richmond. Marijuana, or "reefer" as we called it, was everywhere then, not that it isn't today, but in the mid-seventies it seemed everyone smoked, if only occasionally. It was the mutual friend we all had, and if I was hanging out with friends, it was usually hanging out too. Smoking that shit was all we needed to make any time together fun. Reefer slowed things down making your perception of things more intense, unlike alcohol that would dull your perception. It rarely slowed my reaction or reflex, but gave things like music or movies or just the blossom of a flower new fascination.

Food, of course, required no thinking, reefer triggered insatiable appetites. We never drank much alcohol, a beer here or there, I cannot remember a single time being "drunk" with those guys. I can remember being very stoned with them many times.

The funny thing about reefer was the fact it made everything funny, at first. In the early use, the slightest glare or the simplest comment would cause a burst of laughter. That laughter would cause laughter and it would soon invite anything . . . a dog or a banana or an old lady walking down the street, into a comical scenario that fed upon itself. After regular use, the feeling can be deep thought, what some might call daydreaming. Again, you're not unaware of what's going on, but thoughts are carried longer, the little things you've rarely considered seem fascinating; what keeps the fly on the wall type of stuff. Later, the feeling develops an easy kind of normality, and that's the problem. You don't feel like you are enjoying yourself unless you are high. It's not like an addiction so much as like having rain on a day you need sunshine, a big disappointment. Then after time, you tend to get paranoid and realize it is counter-productive, aside from the damage any smoke will do, you can see what the lethargy does to your progress in life. Hopefully, one realizes this sooner than later and, as with myself, Buck and Battle, and most of my close friends then, you move on and grow.

My friend, Battle, (his last name) as we called him, was from Panama. He had moved to Richmond to live with his aunt and uncle. He had a strong accent and a loud lengthy laugh. We would get high on weekends and hang out in his red and white 1966 Rambler. He had been on the football team and became a close friend. Battle was a little infatuated with white girls, and one Saturday night we drove out to a white party in Hanover County. We had a small bag of reefer and enjoyed a party at the home of a friend of a friend from our high school. Of course, the smoking was discreet and not everybody did it, mostly the white kids wanted to drink, Budweiser and Jack Daniels. We didn't really expect any action with the girls there, but we tried to be "cool" and hope against hope. With a "buzz" going, just seeing those white girls act out with the alcohol was a thrill. We left the party around midnight, and I had Battle laughing as I described the way I was toying with the women. I was, needless to say, bullshitting. He would later call me

"Casanova" as a nickname. We drove back to Richmond on Route 1, not an interstate but a quick two-lane road without traffic. Battle was proud of his little red Rambler, as dinky and dull as it was. He would have the worst air-fresheners hanging on the rear-view mirror. Listening to the static drowning the music on the AM radio station, and chuckling about the white boys at the party, we eventually settled into quiet meditation. We might have been high, but we shook our heads at the thought of some of the guys at that party, full of whiskey staggering about and, unfortunately, even driving. Battle, a Christian Scientist, didn't drink, and I had had less than a beer, so we were careful and comfortable in his old bucket of a car humming down Route 1.

Then, as if he was smacked in the back of the head, Battle sat up with alarm "Oh shit, its da man," he said softly in his distinct accent. At the same moment, I felt the sweep of blue lights across the windshield. "Gotdamn cops, whatda hell we gonna do man, you got dat shit man!" It was a very small bag of reefer, but a bag no less, and I looked around trying to think where I could put it. Meanwhile, the blue lights got closer and Battle is ready to have a baby, "Fuuuck . . . my Auntie's gonna have my ass . . . throw dat shit out da window!" I knew if the cop saw that, it was over. I reached around the base of the seat and found that old Rambler had a split cushion under the seat cover. I slid the reefer into the foam slot where I felt it would be safe, short of a sniffing dog. "Be cool man, be cool," I told Battle while I tried to sit up and lean over at the same time to hide the shit. Battle pulled the car over on the lightly traveled road, only our headlights and the lights of a county police cruiser indicating any life. We could hear our heartbeats as I continued to feel at the bag and cushion to make sure it was in place. The door closed on the cruiser behind us and our hearts raced at three times the speed of the feet approaching.

Small areas of light danced across the inside of the Rambler looking for reason. While we took a deep breath, we heard the words . . . "Can I see your license and registration please?" The officer was typical, tall with a pressed blue uniform, black patent leather belt and a stiff flat-brimmed hat cocked forward on his head far enough to give the impression of a bull about to charge. He stood slightly behind Battle's ear and didn't say a word while Battle reached around for his documents. We had not smoked in the car or had any alcohol at the party, so it's not likely we smelled or appeared drunk, we hoped. The officer looked at Battle's license and pointed his long flashlight around the inside of the car. "Mr. Battle, is this your car?" he asked. Battle, who usually seemed to smile no matter what, was nervous but calm. "Yes sir, it is in my aunt's name, but it is my car . . . she paid for it." I tried not to look at the officer, hoping he wouldn't read my mind, because all I could think about was the bag under my ass. The officer stepped back and looked at the car, probably thinking how few Ramblers were still on the road, then walked back to his cruiser. Battle and I didn't say much while we sat there, just a whisper every second or two of "shiiit, damn", probably going through some mild shock. I just kept thinking . . . please don't ask us to get out of the car.

The officer came back and slowly leaned forward putting his arms on the door. "Do you know how fast you were going Mr. Battle?" Battle squirmed in his seat, "I didn't think I was speeding, is the speed limit 55?" The officer paused a moment, "Yes, it is, but you were doing 40, do you realize that?" My eyes rolled up and I thought, Kiss My Ass . . . we were going too damn slow, Gaahhhddamn. It was a lonely road with few cars to judge speed, but still, we must have been fucked up. "Does your aunt know you are out here tonight?" the officer asked. "Yes sir, we, ah, she always makes sure she knows dat, where I am, officer." Battle went on to tell him that he was from Panama and he lived with his aunt and we were on our way home from a friend's house. Now, I could be cynical and say that if Battle had been alone or had he been with another apparently black male it might have gone differently, but the officer told us to be careful and understand driving too slow sometimes can be unsafe as well.

Perhaps, and probably, he felt we didn't seem a risk so he let us go on. "Thank you, sir, thank you thank you officer, we'll be careful . . . ok, have a good night . . . I will tell my aunt what you said . . . have a good night . . . thank you" Battle replied effusively, practically keeping the officer from leaving. We sat there silently, while we waited for him to pull off. The officer left his lights on while he urged us back on the road. We made sure we did 55mph, not a mile over or under. When we felt ourselves return to normal, we started to laugh about every moment of the event . . . he talking about my stiff actions and digging under the seat, me ridiculing his "Uncle Tom" demeanor . . . "yaa sa, dis my aunt's cah sa, she paid fo it, she always know wha I is sa . . . ain't no drugs n discah sa." The relief of escaping any trouble can trigger laughter but for us, from this, it erupted endlessly until we made it back. That night both of us, with tears from laughter, learned a lesson about pot. And with that, profusely thanked our guardian Angel on Route 1.

Working on road construction the summer after high school was a good job. It paid a decent wage and you got off mid-afternoon. However, before you did, it was real work to endure not just the labor but a slow roast in the sun. The heat on the street can be so intense it bends the light, creating the illusion of water, blending the horizon into itself, while you sweat as if you are but a shelf for the water as well. Mornings came very early, you had to be on site at 7am, a cool time of day that could be so endearing, the stillness of everything but the chatter of birds, the creeping color in the sky, and the fresh taste of the air. Those serene moments passed quickly before I got to the stretch of road being constructed in northern Henrico County. A flat dusty plane of dirt and earth, it reminded me of a moonscape with sporadic craters and mounds dotted with sticks and string.

I worked with a crew of good 'ole boys, mostly teens to early twenties. The foreman was in his late forties with a belly like Bull Conner, the infamous Birmingham police chief, and, I would learn, a brain like his. It was apparent my first day that if you were black you pulled the hardest work. As the white boys stood around the sticks and made measurements, tied string guides for the heavy machinery or held flags to control traffic, the handful of black men were in ditches with shovels and picks. When they were not digging or transporting heavy materials, they were operating something called a tamper. The tamper was a gas-operated machine that packed or "tamped" the dirt. It was like a one leg hopping dancer, bouncing up and down on a piston about two feet long with a small lawn mower engine on top. The base was a flat steel plate that if it hit a foot or toe you had better have steel tip shoes. You would hold on to two bars on the top and try not to let it get away while you guided it. The guys would alternate this through the day because the vibration could wear you out after an hour or so.

My job, yes, was to hold the flags for traffic and do the things the white boys did. In other words, be white. Because we worked in groups, it meant being around the white guys. I talked with them some, but mostly listened. The conversation could be about the usual stuff young men speak of . . . sports, girls, cars, and girls. Once, they talked about black people, I don't remember them using the word nigger, but they joked about the "Steppin Fetchit" type they liked. "Yeah, I like'em when they're big and black and they sweat" one of them said. He was a tall, frail redneck that would have hardly said that anywhere but among buddies. It drew amused chuckles from his coworkers, as it left me resentful, and ashamed I did not respond. It went on for a few more chuckles and then the subject left the conversation as casually as it came. They didn't know I was black, and to make it known at that point could have caused a blow up because the other black guys would have found out what they said. I didn't want to jeopardize the job, for any of us, so I did what I had done far too many times in the past, just let it go. I knew I could probably kick any one of their asses if it came to it, but as the saying goes . . . you have to pick your battles.

A few days later, I arrived for work, grabbed a set of flags, and assumed I would handle traffic duty. "Richardson!, come here" the foreman gruffed. He walked toward me huffing and puffing like I had made some stupid blunder. "Put those flags back and get over here!" he said with disgust. I walked behind him feeling the eyes of my coworkers as he led me to the trench where the brothers were gathering tools for the heavy labor ahead. "Go'on down there and get onea'em show you how to run dat tamper." The brothers looked up at me and at each other wondering what the hell I must have done. It was never said, of course, but it was not what I had done, it was what I had become. In less than a week, the word had passed that I was black. In their eyes, I had passed for white, which turned the red on their necks a new shade. The attitude toward me from that foreman seemed to obsess him; I could do no right and found myself each evening with a tingling in my arms from the hours holding that tamper. The upside was the friendship I gained from the brothers in the trench; as was always, black folk were not nearly as surprised as the whites. They would have plenty of laughs about it, "Yeah, you thought you were slick . . . shiiid, you remember next year nigga" referring to a line from Richard Pryor, the great comedian of the seventies. They would also imitate the foreman, finding things to laugh about while the dust and sun and "Bull Conner" poured over us.

Lunchtime was only twenty minutes each day, and each day, we pushed it down to allow a few minutes to rest and sometimes nap. One day I fell asleep in my car and "Bull" pounded on the window. "You think you getting paid to sleep, I be damned!" he growled. I jumped up. For the next hour, he hovered over me looking for a reason to bark. "Don't do it like that, damnit!" . . . "Go get that shovel, hurry up!" I imagined what a chain gang was like, all of this plus chains and brutality. I didn't see myself lasting the summer, it was obvious that clown had a special disdain for me. One day he bitched about something I was doing and said, "Am I gonna have to wipe yo ass after lunch?" The white boys laughed as if on command, sucking up to him. Between the hard work, and bitter moments like that, I thought to myself another line from Richard Pryor, "well fuck it then" I dropped my shovel and looked at him, "Naw, you gonna have to kiss my ass after lunch," I said. I jumped from the hole and walked away as everyone seemed to hold their breath and sweat. "That's fine, you lucky I'm on the job, get out of here" he yelled, almost shivering.

It had been so overt, so obvious. One day I'm just another kid, the next day I was the target of sarcasm or silence from most of the whites, and shit from that asshole. The experience was a version of something not new, but now, I was pretty much an adult. When I was growing up I would say to myself "yeah, guilty as charged, I know, you can't believe I'm black, go ahead stare . . . I'm getting used to it." I was a kid with a kind of handicap, the difference only that it was not evident, it had to be learned. Now, it seemed I was expected to make it known the moment we meet: "Hi, I'm Monte, nice to meet you . . . I know you think I'm white, but I'm black . . . no joke." Then, there would be no sense of betrayal later, no shock to the narrative.

Those rednecks on that road crew took it personally, unlike a child or young teen might, they believed I had a responsibility to provide opportunity to their prejudice. This was a new dynamic, the "don't ask, don't tell" way would not work in the grownup world. Most adults, after some time with me, could discern something ambiguous, or hidden, but rarely gave voice to that aura of caution I could feel from them. I was learning I should try to make my blackness more apparent, for white folk especially, to allow, at least, some uncertainty. There was frustration in that daily life as a young man, and even today to an extent at times, feeling like I was always in an involuntary disguise. The constant awareness of this "disguise" became more profound as adulthood changed social interactions. I was becoming me, no longer a kid in a bizarre place feeling like an innocent victim, but slowly I acquired a more confident and dignified projection of yes, this is me, I deal with it, now you deal with it.

Six

By the fall, it was school time. Virginia Commonwealth University is located in the center of Richmond. A liberal arts and medical college, it was a center of freethinking, progressive students with a nationally recognized art and design program. VCU was not the school I imagined going to. I hoped that I might play college ball and maybe even make it to the pros, but VCU didn't have a real football team, didn't have a real track team, only a basketball program, which has become very successful. I could have gone to a smaller school to play football, but given the financial circumstance, VCU was right because I was good in art. What a new world, even though I was living at home, I had a sense of independence but also felt part of a group as a "VCU Ram." I didn't feel so unique for the first time, all the students were "doing their own thing", clothes, hair styles, music, politics, drugs, sex, food, it was all being perceived anew. Anything that you might think strange was simply something that had not been explained yet. So like most colleges, it was all about exposure to ideas, ideas that manifest themselves in expressions that only young adults dare portray. VCU has one of the finest art programs in the country, music and performing arts, along with design and photography. I majored in Commercial Art, but I don't believe I felt passionate about my direction. I was just going with the flow, and marijuana has a way of making you do just that.

My early classes were in design and color and art history. The first few weeks we practiced contrast and shading, and one of the primary forms to know, the human body. Models, of course, were there many days to allow us practice on the incredibly subtle variations of the face, and often, nudity for body knowledge. As young kids right out of high school, you can imagine the atmosphere in class the first time. Everyone realizing that we are now supposedly adults, and so no giggles or wide eyes, but it was certainly odd. Even more so, during the times we had Janice. Like most models, Janice was either a student or just a young person earning a few extra dollars to take off his or her clothes for the viewing of strangers. However, this was for "art," no shame or stigma of a dancer to excite drunken men, though some may have done both. Janice, however, surely did it for art sake. Important in illustration is contrast, and with the human body, Janice provided excellent practice. The first time she came in it was obviously going to be different and the giggles required additional restraint. Janice was about 350lbs. The folds, curves, and deep dark lines of contrast were perfect to demonstrate how light works and contrast changes. It also gave everyone more perspective on this young woman, and those like her, who live with bodies that otherwise would never be considered works of art. Janice had grace and dignity, and while she understood the attention she received carried little if any lust, the overwhelming currency of any nineteen-year-old, she seemed proud that her form, in those moments, was appreciated and valued. She had an impact on us beyond her size. I certainly don't recall a single other model from those days. They were just another pretty face.

"Boy, you look like some wild bear!" my mother would say when my hair got long and full. "That's a durn shame . . . if you don't look like a mess I don't know what to say." It was red, bushy and bright, a kind of flame on my head. When I ran, it would bounce like a pillow flopping on my shoulders. Of course, I would have a "Pick" comb to bring it to its full glory. Most picks were tall with plastic handles and long straight metal "teeth." They would come in all colors, shapes, and motifs, but the one everybody had regardless of any others was the 'Black Power' fist, a clinched fist atop the handle of a black comb that would rise above the "fro" like the black leather gloved fist thrust in the air by John Carlos in Mexico City during the 1968 Olympics. The image was so iconic, so inspirational, that few large afros lacked the upheld fist. However, I rarely wore it, especially around strangers. "Who the hell that white boy think he is . . . tryin' to act all black, better take dat shit out his head!" That response was predictable and understandable, so I just saved myself the unnecessary friction. My sense of identity was that of being black in a very unique way. I was as black as any young man my age, except in appearance. That said, I was perhaps not as Black as any other young man. Walking through America with dark skin I cannot speak to. And yet sometimes I think it's easier when you know what others perceive you as, even if you know it could be extremely detrimental, because you don't have to read or calculate the consequence at every new counter, be it Black or White.

Certainly, the spectacle that was me, was still unique even at VCU. But here my peers saw me as just another "wow" moment in their day. It was usually not too bad, but still it was a big change from high school. The issue of my race seemed more of a fascination or curious adventure for some. I guess part of the wild nature of youth. That wild nature in the mid-seventies was evident all over, everyone was encouraged to "do their own thing" and be "natural," not having "hang-ups" about traditional things. It created an atmosphere of fearlessness about social activities, and women could be pretty social. It was quite a leap from high school, it seemed some girls, and men for that matter, were not so tethered by the identities they had to maintain growing up, whether of class or race or even culture. I suppose most eighteen-year-olds have a somewhat petulant reaction to being "free," doing things simply because it is an exercise in independence. Still, it also allows more real, you might say mature, engagement. Those engagements, whether sexual or otherwise, helped me grasp a better feel about people. I saw more and more whites that were willing to, at least, try and be friends with blacks and share something. Given the terrible racial history, it took courage to acknowledge fault to pursue friendship, and not just the "yeah yeah, we made you slaves, let's get pass it" demeanor that many took. But maybe it was at times simply me. Simply seeing how complicated and unnecessary this whole notion of skin color and race shaped America.

At VCU, I met a real girl-friend, Shelly. She was a real friend, not a sex mate. Blonde and blue-eyed, she had a confident poise and a dimpled child-like smile. She was in a couple of my art classes and we became good friends, although she had a boyfriend back home. We seemed to have a connection that went beyond a physical thing, a true friendship. As art students, we would spend many days outside simply drawing what we saw. Shelly and I would always find ourselves laughing or talking about "life." I suppose she may have thought I was Jewish initially, as she was, and finding out I was Black was, of course, a surprise. "You want to go see "Grease" together?" She actually asked me on a date. "Grease" was the movie with John Travolta and Olivia Newton John. "Yeah, let's go" I said while thinking, "wow!" It was a kind of formal invitation of public companionship, something rare up until then. Sure, there had been girls, but none had ever offered to be seen as my "partner," officially so to speak, in public. There would be other movies and other days spent together, museums, drawing scenes of life in the "Fan," the district in Richmond that much of VCU occupied. We would just hang out and enjoy each other at places we both enjoyed like the old historic train station on Broad Street, Union Station.

We loved to skateboard, it was the one thing we did most. Often in Maymont Park, where the walkways were wide and hills sloped gently. Skateboarding was popular with lots of young people and we were good at it. I still have that very skateboard forty years later. She and I went to museums and explored historical parts of Richmond, doing the things couples do. We spent long evenings together and kissed, but it never went beyond that. She held true to herself and I would not push things. It was fine; she held nothing from me otherwise and provided the most endearing memories for me at VCU. I even helped her move her things back to McLean for the summer with my dad's truck, meeting her parents and spending the night there. To look back, it is interesting that the first white girl to truly allow me in her world was Jewish, not having the heritage, in a way, of the average white person. Perhaps, or perhaps not, had I been dark-skinned she might have had second thoughts, considering public scrutiny, but the fact I was black in all things but appearance had no negative to her. She didn't return to VCU that fall, transferring to another school and we fell out of touch. In 2012, I was curious and found her on the internet. She was living in Houston as an artist decorator, divorced with two daughters. We exchanged a couple emails and I said I would call so we could speak for the first time in 35yrs. I never did, afraid perhaps of corrupting my idea of who she was. I don't know why, because I really hope she has had a good life.

Today, when I think about those couple of years they seem more like five or six, so many experiences with family, buddies, school, reefer, and women. I suppose it is that way for everyone when they think of their youth, before the routine of jobs and people and shit that happens start to blur the years. There were many especially fun times with my cousin Bill. Bill Greene and I were very close for a few years at the end of high school and after. We would often talk about a wide range of things, from science to politics to cars. He was about seven years older but we "clicked" like twins; in fact, Bill had an identical twin, Walter. Once, the three of us were riding in his '72 Chevelle laughing about all the crazy stuff we observed and Bill remarked how weird he felt. He leaned back from the steering wheel with his broad grin and chuckled, "Man, this is freaky, we're all talking trash and goin' on bout shit and I look in the mirror . . . and there's this white boy in the back seat . . . damn." He and Walter laughed with a kind of pride, as if they were privy to secrets of the universe. I laughed too, it was weird, and I did feel like an unusual, if not special, product of the universe.

Bill had perspective on things I found at times brilliant, with a strong knowledge of black history. He could often put things in an ironic context, to which I could relate. We would often amuse ourselves with the reaction of others when they realized I was black. Bill's blackness was another case. He was stocky and strong, with a broad nose, full lips, dark skin and beard. It was fascinating to see how white people saw him, like the stereotype . . . a big brute they should avoid, when the reality was he was a smart, kind, and gentle man. One should never judge a book by its cover, as the saying goes, especially if you plan to burn it.

Bill's wit and humor, his strong yet unpretentious intellect, with a very easy-going approach to life, in hindsight I believe rubbed off on me. Bill was usually my "go to" man about things, particularly women. He in fact brought me into an eye opening world of older women his age. Bill is from the Greene side of my family; his grandfather was the brother of my grandmother, Amanda Greene, who married Charlie Richardson. His grandmother, Alice, had outlived her husband by many years and lived with Bill and his parents for as long as I remembered. Grandma Alice was one of my favorite people, always with a smile and always with witful wisdom. As a young woman with Black and American Indian blood, I was told, she was a striking beauty. Aunt

Alice would always be sitting at the kitchen table reading, or preparing food. It was not unusual to hear Aunt Alice say words in a mixed quizzical way. She might say something like, "I used to have a garden with lots of pee-el-ants," (plants) or "we need to pick up some ef el ours for your mother". Other times she might be forgetful and say "it hit a slick spot," the thought, she said, slipped off her brain. Her sayings had an artistic intelligence about them, some might describe as quirky or odd, often seeing things from "outside the box." I miss her perspective, and the happiness it seemed to provide her.

My brother Chuck and his wife, Phyllis, lived in Byrd Park, a section of the west end. They had a small brick home where we would watch things like the Super Bowl and other sporting events, hang out, and listen to the music of Marvin Gaye, Freddie Hubbard or Eddie Harris. One afternoon, I was over there drooling over his new Maraantz stereo system and looking at some of his many albums. Albums are not used today, everything is digital and kept on an Mp3 player, but back in the seventies, for those too young to know, there were vinyl records that we played on turntables. The albums came in protective cardboard sleeves or 'album covers' that provided all the information about the songs and artists, etc. The covers were also works of art, often elaborate designs or photography. The firm flat sides of the album covers were also the perfect plane to clean the seeds from marijuana (reefer), often, the prep for your favorite music. Chuck and I debated the new Grover Washington album "Mister Magic," whether it was better than "Breezin" from George Benson, which had been out a few months. Chuck thought "Mister Magic" was better, but I said it was no contest. "Breezin is dynamite, all the songs are good . . . it's gonna be classic, watch" I nodded a negative about Grover's new thing.

Chuck leaned back and kind of nodded in agreement but he wasn't paying attention. He sat and stared out the window a few seconds, his mind was somewhere else, he was not high though, Chuck rarely smoked anymore and I was actually over to help him with some yard work. He would give me an "uh huh , yeeeaa . . ." but he was thinking about something else. Out of nowhere he says, "I think I'm gonna declare." I thought to myself, "Man, is he that broke, declaring bankruptcy?" "Bankruptcy?" I asked him silently, looking at him a bit bewildered. His brow slanted and he looked at me. "Naawww man, I'm gonna run for council, city council, I'm gonna declare my candidacy." "Really, you serious?"

It was not something he had talked about before, even as vocal as he was, the thought of running for office never came up. However, the fall of 1976 brought a new ruling from the Justice department. Richmond had to draw new districts and the five 'at large' districts did not fairly represent the large areas of African American voters. There would now be nine. This opened up new races, and the fifth district, Chuck's district, was the key. Of the nine new districts, it was almost certain that four winners would be black, including two incumbents, and four would be white. The fifth district was the swing district. It featured some of the most classic and beautiful homes in Richmond, including those on Monument Ave. and the beautiful Byrd Park. It had a very diverse population, both racially and economically. With three black contenders and a white candidate with strong business support, it was crucial that the black vote not be split. With a black councilman from the fifth, Richmond would have its first majority black council, and likely, the first black mayor, since the council selects a mayor. That fall, there was a strong effort to register voters and find a candidate, including a move to support Chuck's father-in-law, Dr. Ford Johnson, a prominent black dentist. 'Doc,' was not interested, but urged Chuck to consider running, as did others from the community. In September, Chuck had lost his job at the Richmond Regional Planning Commission, and with 'fate to the wind' bravado, at twenty-eight, hit the street. He walked virtually every neighborhood, meeting and wining over young and old, black and white.

He ran . . . and he won! In 1977, by twelve votes, the capital of the confederacy, Richmond, would see its first majority black council. The history of that election cannot be understated. This was The capital of the confederacy, a place where black people had been, until a century before, enslaved for well over two hundred fifty years. Now, the great grandchildren of slaves would run this once citadel of southern life. This would be the fruit of not just the adherence to our constitution, but a hundred years effort of diligent blacks and good, principled white folk. Chuck's slogan, "Accountable

Representation," was emblematic of the election; now blacks could believe city government would answer to them as well. The new council, with a five-four majority, would select the first black mayor of Richmond, Henry Marsh.

Chuck was by far the most dynamic on the new council, a Vietnam vet, young and handsome with long flowing black hair and stylish sideburns. Appearing much like the main character in the early seventies movie "Superfly," he was soon a kind of pop star. In the following decade or so, Chuck would become a legend for political and personal reasons. His passion to represent and articulately defend his constituency stood out on council. Only an artificial passion, introduced to him in Vietnam, would be able to unseat him from office. As it had with many in that war, heroin came home with the councilman. It was something I never realized for many years. It is a long and hard story best told by Chuck, and certainly a book in itself, but ultimately he was entrapped by federal agents and spent time in jail, again, a long story. Thankfully, he has been clean over twenty years. The lessons of war, drugs, politics, human frailty, and strength, so poignant in Chuck's story, remain deep in our family.

Seven

"Hi, Maynard Jackson, how are you, good to meet you" spoke the tall handsome figure in our kitchen one sunny Sunday afternoon. This was not just another visitor with my sister Valerie, outside there was a new black Lincoln Continental with two well-dressed 'tough guys' in the front seat . . . bodyguards. This Maynard Jackson was the Maynard Jackson, the first African American mayor of a major southern city, Atlanta. The young political star, of national stature, walked through our small home smiling broadly, as we tried not to be in awe. Valerie was dating and, apparently, very serious about this impressive and eloquent politician. After finishing her graduate degree at the Wharton School of Business in Philadelphia, Valerie got a job in New York City at Grey Advertising. She met Roberta Flack, the very popular singer, and it was at a party thrown by her that she met people like Quincy Jones and this new star of American politics. Maynard, on this day, was not the overweight baby-faced challenger in playful green trunks that knocked down Muhammad Ali in an exhibition. This image in Jet Magazine was well-known in the mid-seventies; but now, Maynard had knocked down his weight as well, and had movie star looks. "Heard a lot about'cha brother" he said to me with a firm handshake and genuine smile. I didn't have much of a response; I was so surprised that a celebrity was actually in our kitchen.

It seemed somewhat surreal, he was almost too big for our little house, not literally, but his presence and aura made everything seem tight and close. If Maynard was here to visit the parents, it must be serious between them. He stayed a while and got to know us, and from the moment he first spoke, it was clear why he was a phenomenon. His charm was genuine, his intellect obvious but not imposing. When he left, we all stood in the kitchen with wide-eyed grins, leaving it to momma to say what she would say at any interchange on this road of life . . . "Lord have mercy." Before anybody could speculate or gossip much, they were getting married. The wedding was in October of 1977 in Richmond, at the home of Chuck's father-in-law Dr. Johnson. The Johnson's home was large and beautiful. Located at the edge of Byrd Park, facing an iconic lake and fountain, it had all the stylings of old affluent Richmond. All I remember is the smiles, everybody was smiling, even the journalists and photographers. It was a moment of transcendence; Between Chuck and Maynard, we were now connected to the political spearhead of the movement. This ultra-light-skinned family, so light-skinned we had to defend our blackness, proved we were really black. We were now not only black, but Black Power! The cliché is probably true . . . "Only in America."

In Atlanta, Valerie was all the rage, the Mayor or "The Maynard" as many called him, had just enjoyed a landslide re-election, lost considerable weight, and won this impressive new bride. It would be a time of profound change for Atlanta, emerging as a new international city, home to more Fortune 500 companies than any other, and becoming what would be called the "Black Mecca" for African American business, it symbolized the turning point in the political impact of black Americans. Much to the credit of Maynard, his courage, policies, and a proud vision, Atlanta has become one of America's great cities, the only great city of the Old South. Sorry, New Orleans.

Those years were very exciting, but also nervous for us. My seventeen-year-old sister, Vicki, was struggling with a very difficult psychiatric condition. In her senior year, she slowly became almost totally unresponsive to things. She would seem to be daydreaming, and at times, softly talk to herself, or us, incoherently. We had no idea what might have caused it, but certainly knew it was serious. At first, doctors wanted to try shock treatments but our family was against it. Fortunately, a German woman took over, and with medication, Vicki, even missing three months of school, fought back to graduate on time. It was hard to see my little sister go through it but she would be fine and recover completely. All the while, my mother was working toward her nursing degree at night. Between the elections, Vicki, night school, and still with two young boys in the house, the late seventies were probably the most intense time in my parent's fifty-five year marriage.

At VCU, I was proud of my brother, and brother-in-law, who represented a political evolution that would bring true "Black Power" to many cities that had been redefined by the white flight of the sixties. However, I never really brought it up as some 'claim to fame.' I was shy about the attention and knew it would render the awkward, if unspoken, issue of how I could be so white yet be so bona fide black. My sophomore year was spent mixing the girls and smoking pot, causing my grades to suffer, leading to academic suspension. It was so foolish of me to lose a semester. Money would also become an issue; the work of commercial art requires materials, things like paint, camera, film, paper, different pencils and pens, but it went beyond that. I could blame it on money or pot, but it was also a lack of discipline that ultimately denied me a degree. That failure has always been an embarrassment, and although it lead me to Atlanta, and I don't think I would change that, I never went back to finish school. I took a couple classes at Mercer University in Atlanta but never earned a degree. How that has affected the welfare of my family since, I am ashamed about.

While I was out of school that fall, Chuck's father-in-law had a house he acquired at auction from the IRS that needed occupation. It had been the home of a convicted drug dealer and it certainly had the look. It had been remodeled with dark maroon siding, black window trim, and a dark tinting on the windows. Doc, as we knew him, needed someone to stay in the house, for insurance purposes, until he could sell it. So I thought what's not to like about that deal, a place to hang out, even if it was the gaudiest place one could imagine. Inside, the walls were covered in red and black crushed Spanish velvet, black trim throughout and red carpet wall-to-wall. It was actually spooky, like Dracula's lair. It was a big house with a basement and two upper floors, and without furniture, and with the dark tones, people would ask if I was scared there alone. Actually, it was a bit unnerving, but I confronted it. On October 31, Halloween, at midnight, I walked through the house, lights out, opening every door. The darkness was absolute, and a couple times, I had to feel along the velvet walls and take deep breaths, believing nothing would happen but not knowing it. It's funny how we like to entertain ourselves with the fear of the supernatural. Of course, it was uneventful, as my cousin Bill had told me beforehand, "there is nothing in the dark that is not in the light." I spent about six months there 'ghost free,' but not alone. For a short while we kept an after-hours "speak easy," selling drinks and playing music down in the full basement. A friend of Chuck's named "Red," set it up and we called it the 'Red Carpet.' My friend Buck and I had several memorable adventures there with the older women that would come by. There were usually only a few people most nights, those who were friends of friends, etc. One night, Chuck brought by a lady with classic Italian or Greek-like features. Her name was Annie.

Annie Reynolds was one of "Chuck's girls." Even though he and Phyllis seemed happy, Chuck would sometimes allow himself to be 'caught' by some of the women that chased him. One weekend, he asked me to take Annie to a small country club west of Richmond so he could meet up with her there. Annie was very soft spoken, to the extent her voice was like a whisper, and she had a kind, innocent personality. That ride sealed the deal; it wouldn't be long before I would start seeing her myself. The dynamics in those times were such that it was not an issue if it was not a true girlfriend, and there was no compunction on their part. Annie was nine years older than me and had a nine-year-old son, Jimmy, from a short-lived marriage at age twenty. Next thing I know, here I am about to start living with an older white woman with a son. Although Annie was from one of those old southern families that would find it an outrage, she was not bothered by their reaction. Living alone and raising a child left her little time to care about their displeasure. She had lived in California for a few years, up north in Humboldt County, notorious for the marijuana farms and hippie lifestyles. She had more than a few stories of the parties where drugs were available on tables like chips and dip. She moved back in 1975 and lived alone with Jimmy in a small house on the north side of Richmond. I found myself with a woman the age of my big brother, with a son the age of my little brother.

We soon found ourselves in the grind of working, cooking, and trying to raise her son. Annie had a special touch when it came to decorating, even with thrown together hand-me-downs and thrift store findings, she could create the most cozy and charming rooms. That winter we couldn't meet the gas bill and found ourselves without heat on one of the coldest nights that year. I remember being huddled in a blanket by the stove, the oven door opened, and on high, as the three of us managed. Jimmy was unfazed. He was generally not very talkative and probably saw me as another one of the men his mother spent time with. He took the cold as he would take almost any hardship, stoic and quiet, as if he knew it would just be a matter of time. Jimmy didn't believe in God, he would say so with a very matter-of-fact calmness that was hard for me to understand. I would try sometimes to talk to him about it, but he'd simply shrug his shoulders like it really did not matter. He was mature beyond his years, probably due to the road he had traveled with his mom as a child. The relationship caused some big issues with Annie's family and she had a strained time with her mother particularly. Annie and I lived in her small house about a year, and then a short while in the Fan District near VCU, in an apartment on Floyd Ave.

Early in 1979, Valerie asked if I would like to move to Atlanta. "Come on down, so I can have some family near me, and you can get back in school." I liked the idea but was unsure about Annie, whether she should, or would come. We had been together almost two years at that point, which seems much longer when you are twenty-two, and I didn't want to end our relationship because I was moving. I decided to go, and to the disappointment of Annie's mother, as well as Valerie, the two of us moved. I would leave a couple weeks ahead of Annie to get started, or I should say get familiar, with the apartment Valerie had already in place. The early morning of May 4th was sunny and mild, spring was in full bloom, and it was time to leave. Annie was upset about leaving Richmond, since she had moved more than a couple times in the last ten years with her son. Jimmy would stay behind with his dad until the fall and she wouldn't see him for several months. We lingered outside a few minutes and I walked around the car going through my pre-trip checklist. Fortunately, my eyes fell on the rear wheel and noticed that all but one of the lug nuts had been removed! Some asshole, from her family I'm sure, wanted to say goodbye in true redneck fashion. I was pissed but felt so lucky I had noticed. It might have been just a delay, falling off in the parking lot as I pulled off, or it could have been tragic had I made it to the interstate. Annie was furious, and was suddenly anxious, to at least, get away from that part of her family. I took one nut from each of the other four wheels and put them on the vandalized rim. We said goodbye and I broke the tether of home. My sister Ruthie would ride with me, so I picked her up and we hit the road. Unsure of everything ahead, but certain of one thing, I'd be followed by the awkward, unnecessary, chronic issue of color.

I had been to Atlanta once before, when we brought down a truckload of items for Valerie after she got married. I came with Ric Lewis, a good friend of mine at the time. Ric and I were 'getting high' buddies and, of course, we did it while driving to Atlanta. We did fine on the road, getting high was so normal for us that it would have been a bummer to make the long boring trip without it. It isn't that pot didn't alter our state, but not in the way alcohol does, blurring and doubling vision or slowing down reaction, it mostly just changed the things we daydreamed about as you daydream on any long road trip. When we arrived at Valerie's, it was pretty exciting. Their apartment was in a high rise at the corner of North and Peachtree Street that looked toward downtown. When I walked in the first time, it was like a curtain being pulled back on a movie. I could almost hear harp strings as the city sparkled beyond a shear, beaded curtain to the balcony. White Scandinavian furniture and fine artwork seem to float in the air as light jazz cooled the sound of the city below. It brought a proud grin to my face. "Check this out" I said with my expression at Ric. It was a new, organic high for both of us.

Moving to Atlanta was far more daunting, not just a new school, it was a real change. The first few weeks, I lived with a good friend of Valerie and Maynard's, and my friend since, Mack Wilbourn. Mack was a successful young entrepreneur, who owned three McDonald's restaurants. He had recently divorced and lived a "fruitful" bachelor life. He had a nice home in the Sherwood Forest neighborhood in midtown, looking out over the Ansley golf course, another reminder of the new level in society I was being exposed to. "OK, I don't know how your day was but it's time to chill," Mack said on one of the first evenings, while he put on music and poured one of his expensive wines. Mack worked hard, spending long days at his restaurants and cultivating business ties, but he also played hard. Those first several weeks with him saw only a few nights that we did not have fun with good drink, good laughs, good music . . . and the company of 'good' girls. My head was spinning by the time I moved out, I didn't cheat on Annie but the idea of what could lie ahead was eye opening.

Afterwards, I initially stayed in an apartment complex near the church Maynard's father was once a preacher, Friendship Baptist Church, on the west side of downtown. I was there just a couple weeks, long enough to have my portfolio stolen from my car. It was foolish that I had left it there; it contained artwork and photography that reflected several years work, and painful to the point of tears, but I certainly matured about living in the big city. Annie moved down in July, much to Valerie's displeasure; I suppose the notion of the first lady's brother living with an older white woman was not the most flattering at the time, but also she probably knew, rightly so, that it would not last. "He brought a sandwich to the banquet!" Mack would say when he talked to others about me. Atlanta, indeed, was overflowing with beautiful Black women, some upwardly mobile, others just very mobile, scouting out the "Mecca" of Black power in America.

Annie and I soon moved to the Virginia Highlands neighborhood, a Bohemian, soon to be very fashionable area at the east end of midtown. I had worked a brief time for a sign company downtown, painting and installing signs, but Maynard arranged an interview with the general manager of the NBC television station.

———

Jeff Davidson, the GM at the NBC affiliate Channel 11, played quite the "big shot." He leaned back in his chair, rolling a burning cigar across his mouth looking around his fancy office, replete with expensive wood and leather, a private bathroom, and even a separate walk-in bar, contemplating the mayor's brother-in-law across the desk. In his mid-forties, he led a TV station at a time when they were money-making machines. As one of the salesmen told me years later, "We would go to lunch with clients and simply pick the highest bidder, a license to steal, the money was easy and endless." Jeff would never have met with someone trying to be hired at an entry-level, but he probably liked the notion of the mayor owing him a favor. "So, what do you see yourself doing in the future?" he asked. "Well, I would like to make movies one day, perhaps cinematography, and maybe being a cameraman would be a good step for me." I wiggled in the chair and tried to get comfortable in the only ill-fitting suit I had. "I like Maynard, I respect him a great deal, I don't always agree with him but I respect him" he said with a grin. Jeff was likable, although full of himself, and said he could at least give me something for the summer and we would see what happens in the fall. It was a very different outcome from the interview a couple days earlier with Paul Raymon, the GM at the CBS affiliate. That visit was glaringly perfunctory. I got about five minutes of half his attention, and left without even empty encouragement.

I started on at Channel 11, classified as something called "casual labor," a category that allowed them broad flexibility on things like overtime and benefits. TV news had become a big player in the major cities, and to be part of a news crew carried a bit of celebrity, so it was a position many could envy. "Do you know what ENG stands for?" asked Joel, one of the technicians who maintained the equipment, as well as assisting as a sound man on the crew. "Electronic News Gathering," he said. I'm sure he must have thought, wow, we're starting from scratch with this guy. I knew little to nothing about it, film and photography were familiar but this was a fairly new beast in the late seventies . . . video. They were transitioning from film to video tape, a change the whole world would make, making the whole world change. About half the photographers still shot 16mm film, as they slowly learned the new system. I began working with Joel, going out on assignments acting as the sound technician. At the time, the equipment was large and heavy, needing two people, along with a reporter. I learned to operate the large videotape recording decks, and be responsible for the audio.

"It beats working for a living" was the refrain from the chief photographer there. It did, each day was like having a ringside seat to almost anything you could imagine, from the most famous to the most infamous, from heartbreaking tragedy to exhilarating excitement; we were witness. I had never flown a day in my life, and here I was, going up in a small helicopter. "Skycam," the first in the Atlanta market, a virtual glass bubble that could carry four, made reaching the scene of events only minutes away. It was utterly amazing, views flying just above the glittering skyline as the sun set with the crisp colors of autumn, or circling a spot like a bird eyeing its prey.

When we swooped down on a scene, it was as if you were a superhero coming to make someone or something a star, everybody would stare and seem to envy what we did. It was fun, and it did seem to beat working for a living, although it could be risky if you allowed yourself to be caught up in the thrill.

Once in the late eighties I was in Skycam shooting a fire. On shoots like that we would remove the lightweight Plexiglas door of the helicopter on the cameraman's side to allow a greater field of view. I was holding the camera in my lap until we arrived on the scene then picked it up to start shooting. The pilot would keep the chopper high enough or upwind to avoid smoke. Often, but not always, photographers would put one foot on the helicopter skid only a foot or so outside the door; it allowed a little better stability when the pilot tilted slightly for the birds-eye view. When I was done and we started back I heard something hitting against the side of the chopper. I didn't notice at first because I was wearing a headset that muffled sound and allowed communication with the pilot. I turned and looked to see what was happening and I saw my seatbelt flapping and smacking the side. Those belts were like something out of a 1968 Chevy, a simple spring release lever that required less than a half inch lift to free. Apparently, when I raised my camera to start shooting, it somehow provided the weak lift needed to leave me unsecured. Kinda scary to think about, huh?

I worked through the summer and fall, and they seemed happy with my progress. The "casual laborer" lasted about nine months, until April, when I took my first flight on a commercial airline to Dallas. They sent me to a Kodak film workshop to learn more about 16mm film processing. Channel 11 had the largest news film processor in the South, and I would get the full-time job of running it. However, it was not for long, film was being phased out and I continued to go out on shoots as an audio technician. The use of film would end in the early eighties, as video became the perfect format for TV news and, as we know today, the ubiquitous tool in everyone's hand. In those early days the technology was allowing so much more production, and the once rare "live" on location broadcasts, would become unremarkable.

For the next year or so I continued as an audio tech, assisting photographers on everything from boring meetings to fires. Ron Loving, one of the station photographers, was my usual partner in those first days. Ron taught me a lot, as did others like Norris Smith, Mike Zakel, Rich Foster and reporters Maynard Eaton and Jon Shirek. I was a virgin to TV news, something unheard of in a major market, and their guidance and goodness was invaluable. Maynard and Valerie knew Ron from his media position, but he had also been an Atlanta police officer. We would sometimes just cruise the streets, especially if the weather was nice, listening to the police scanners. One beautiful afternoon we heard a call for police and fire rescue at a Georgia Power substation, someone had climbed up onto the high voltage structure. When we got there the police had blocked all traffic but let us through, telling us to remain out of sight as best we could. The person sitting forty feet up on the crossbars of this maze of wires, six-foot transformers and capacitors, was a young teenager. We made our way across the street and stood behind a large tree. Ron peered around one side with his camera as I squatted and looked from the other. The boy threatened to jump and would not to respond to officers. He sat there leaning forward with his head down, occasionally looking up as if asking himself what to do. It was the first time I found myself in the awkward position of professional gawkier. I felt the curious fascination we all have at something like that, but also, had the obligation to "see it" for others. It meant being aware of everything, from police and rescue activity to the shifts in the wind.

We sat behind the tree for almost an hour, Ron rolling video almost every moment. We didn't want to miss the boy falling, even though it was very unlikely we would air it, but at the same time, our stomachs twisted from the thought of seeing it. The police brought the teen's mother to the scene, and from directly below, she pleaded and cried as he wiggled above her. The deep rumbling of fire trucks trying to position a ladder, at times, drowned out the words from mother to son. There was no room for a truck to get to him and it was clear he would have to come down on his own. I looked through the camera that zoomed in to the point you could see the tortured look on the boy. Somehow, by fear or courage, he slowly started to slide along the beam, and came down. "Oh well, let's get outta here" Ron said casually, slinging the camera over his shoulder. I was still trying to process the intensity of the last hour while he moved with the routine of just another day, just another day. It was the life of a news photographer.

It would become almost routine over the years to find yourself in the midst of drama or some sort of fascination, meeting famous people and hundreds of normal folk that for good, bad, ugly or sad reasons, we put on TV. The early years also exposed me to some of the "Knights" of the civil rights movement. I knew of a few like Hosea Williams, Andy Young, Coretta Scott King and John Lewis, but I would be at many press events with people like C.T Vivian, Joseph Lowery, James Orange, Hank Thomas, Joe Boone, people who had been Freedom Riders and marchers on the front lines in the sixties. It was Atlanta after all, only a decade or so after MLK.

Eight

During that time in Atlanta, everyone was consumed by the case of the "missing and murdered children". Young black males were being found dead, usually asphyxiated, around mostly black communities, or often dumped in the Chattahoochee river on the west side of town. Ultimately, almost thirty boys and young men were found between mid 1980 to late 1981. In some areas, young men formed self-proclaimed security patrols. Maynard, as mayor, would feel a burden and frustration few politicians could imagine. The city was offering over a million dollars in cash for an arrest and conviction. All kinds of theories and conspiracies weighed the talk from bars to boardrooms, yet police were without many leads. The murders seemed to happen almost weekly. "What a nightmare . . . it got to the point I hated to hear the phone ring," Maynard said years later. It was intense for everyone, as people looked twice at those around them. We were living at a place called "The Colonnades" near the intersection of Ponce de Leon and Highland Ave. An old, once elegant, pair of buildings separated by a courtyard, it had three levels supported by large antebellum columns. Our unit was on the third and top floor, and our balcony faced the same type unit across the yard. The neighbor directly across from us was a burly, muscular black man named Malcolm.

Malcolm was in his late forties and lived alone, and although friendly, there was something odd about him. He would sometimes say things that didn't make sense and then look at you for a reaction, often giggling or bending a coy smile. He was not as tall as me, but he was stout, and bald, and his demeanor could sometimes create an uneasy feeling. Like everybody, at times we talked about the murders, and he would say things like "you know, pharaoh wanted all the male babies killed, it's kinda like that, like the bible say." We thought it was weird, but that was the kind of stuff Malcolm said. He worked the overnight shift at an industrial bakery on the south side and often bragged how he was able to go without much sleep. "When I was in the army I had special training . . . I can't tell you about that though, it's top secret" he mentioned a few times with a devious chuckle. He had served twenty years in the army, in places like Alaska and the Philippines, according to him, on special missions. He showed us his military I.D from the late fifties like some claim to fame. One afternoon he came by for some reason and told us he was going to take some boys from the YMCA, or some shelter, I don't remember, to a Braves baseball game. He said he would sometimes help as a "big brother" for a church he attended. He had a bag with him with binoculars and other things for the game, and also in the bag, a handgun. He pulled it out and showed it to us, "it's for protection, you never know with these murders going on," he said. We were, to say the least, surprised and very disturbed. We asked him to put the gun away; we were not necessarily afraid, but it was uncomfortable.

Given his character, we became very suspicious from that point. Again, at the time, everybody was leery of strange behavior. We said to ourselves, maybe he is the child killer, or maybe working with the child killer, there are just too many things about him. His overnight shift on the side of town where many of the kids lived, his strength, the weird things he said about the murders, living alone, military training, and now the gun. Everybody would take second looks at anyone that acted even a little strange, but we started to think it could really be possible. Moreover, a thousand weird people live in every city, but he had method to his weirdness, a pattern that was just too hard to brush off.

One day we were talking and he told us that sometimes people just refer to him as "M." "Yeah, sometimes I just go by M, yeah, I think I'm just gonna call myself 'M' he told us, with his usual testing glare. "What do you think, you think you can call me that?" he said. I didn't really give it much thought, just his latest rambling, yeah M for Malcolm, whatever. A couple of weeks later I was glancing through the TV guide and saw a title called "M." I read it, and almost choked, shit on myself, and freaked out at the same time. "M" was the title of a movie made in Germany back in the thirties about a serial child killer in Berlin! That was it . . . fuck the bullshit, I called Valerie and told her about him. My head was spinning thinking about how very possible it was. The Atlanta police were getting hundreds of calls from people suspicious about everyone from neighbors to policemen themselves, but I had the mayor's ear. We didn't know how we should act toward Malcolm from that point, not sure for a few days if or when the police might come to see us, or him. How would we know if he realized they were watching him, or if they talked to him, would he think about his neighbors first? Valerie could not say exactly when they would come by to question him, but told us the day it should happen, Sunday. We tried not to be obvious that day but at least one of us would be on the balcony the whole morning into the afternoon, watching the courtyard, and his apartment directly across from us, anticipating.

Early in the afternoon, the sun lit his building causing a shadow on his balcony, making it harder to see in his apartment, but we could see enough. Annie and I were so spooked we couldn't sit still. We had convinced ourselves he was the child murderer, and were afraid of what might happen over there. Around mid-day, two white men in plain suits, without ties, walked through the courtyard and into his building. They had to be police, no doubt, and we were practically bouncing like nervous cats, looking out the corner of our eyes. The minutes that followed were extremely surreal; we were literally living the scene from Alfred Hitchcock's "Rear Window," as Jimmy Stewart watched Raymond Burr walk through his apartment to answer the door, surprised by police. We watched Malcolm slumber pass the large balcony window to his door. The same silent motions in the movie played in real life across from us. Malcolm turned and walked back into his living room followed by the two detectives. He sat down, but they stood. We could imagine the conversation only, as in the movie, the sounds of traffic, people, and life on a Sunday afternoon was all we heard. I imagined Malcolm grinning while he assuaged the officers with tales of his military background, or perhaps he was nervous and stuttered. And, just like Jimmy Stewart in the movie, we backed away into our shade, feeling the glance, real or not, of Malcolm toward us.

We whispered to each other all the "what ifs," what if they leave without taking him or searching the apartment, what if he comes over after they go, what if he leaves and doesn't return? The officers stood the entire time casually looking around the room, spending about twenty minutes there.

Malcolm never left his seat but he leaned forward and back constantly. When they left, we ducked out of sight and peered through a curtain, watching back and forth between the casual stroll of the two "suits" and Malcolm's apartment. Malcolm walked back, just as casually, across the window and out of sight. After a few minutes, he closed his curtains and doors, preventing any further intrusion of eyes. After that, we didn't see him for several anxious days. The police did not return to our knowledge, and even though they may have watched him for a time, it seemed our suspicion was not useful. Malcolm, from that point, became much less sociable and only spoke briefly to any of his neighbors. Maybe he was just fucking with us, playing a game of sort, psychological warfare from his "secret military work" . . . yeah, right.

Early in 1982, Wayne Williams was arrested, and later convicted of two of the child murders. The other twenty-five were basically attributed to him as well. It left many victims' families, and others, unconvinced he acted alone. Some still believe Williams was not the killer. To this day, I would not be surprised if Malcolm had some involvement, but he was likely just a strange character, highlighted by the strange times.

At the station I was still working as a sound technician and going out every day on assignments for the six o'clock news. Like many businesses, we would hire interns during the summer, and they often would ride along to observe and learn about the daily routines of a TV newsroom. One of those interns was a beautiful young woman from Turkey, here with her husband who was working on his doctorate at Georgia Tech. Her name was Birnur Koca. She had studied journalism in Ankara and wanted to work in television. Birnur would join us often, and soon she and I would find ourselves laughing with each other much of the day. Birnur was a Middle-Eastern beauty, olive skin and almond shaped eyes, rich dark hair and a stunning petite body with the most beautiful legs I've ever seen. She was married, yes, but it was not unlike my relationship with Annie, weak and unrealistic. We became good friends, finding common thoughts about many things. She was surprised I knew so much about Turkey. She said so many people would ask her silly questions like "do they have cars in Turkey?" or "do you see lots of camels . . . where is Turkey?" I had always been curious about other people and other histories, I guess trying to take some stock in my own ambiguous ancestry. As the summer came to an end, I told her I would throw a going away party when she had to leave. She did go back to Turkey for a short while, but I never threw the party, and not long after returning, she was hired by the station. There would be no farewell party.

Late in the summer of '82, I was given the chance to begin shooting news on my own. It was an overnight shift that would have me listening to scanners for things like fires or shootings. We were the first station to cover overnight events, and I was only the second photographer to do it. The first was also a sound tech turned cameraman, who only did it a few months before leaving for a job in Dallas. I often spent much of the night riding around town, observing empty scenes locked in an eerie glow of pale yellow streetlights, the only movement perhaps a stray dog or the change of traffic signals. Thirty years later those same streets are full of life at 2 am, but not then.

There were times it was very serene, a softness that belied the concrete and steel, yet, edgy as I listened for police or fire calls. Most nights had me covering bad events but occasionally I would do a piece on the other folks that worked when most slept. The baker or perhaps the dairy farmer outside of town, the road crews on the highway and even the homeless looking for things of value. But, mostly, it was spent like the overnight crews today, chasing ambulances. Getting to the scene quickly was crucial, and I soon learned, when to leave quickly as well. One night I responded to a shooting at a club in the west end, a hole in the wall speak-easy, where alcohol bred bravado and violence. I was there as the paramedics loaded the victim and the police talked to witnesses. I shot the ambulance driving away and the police as they did the same. When I turned to walk back to my car, I realized there was only me on the scene, with those drunk and mad bar patrons. They were still energized by the shots and police and blood, and turned their attention to me. They said a few sarcastic words and looked resentful about the TV camera with its white cameraman. I learned that night never to let myself be the last one around at a time and place like that. They talked loudly and watched me load my gear. And while I left without incident, I took with me an important lesson.

Life with Annie was becoming more difficult. She was always suspicious of other women and we talked less and less. We rarely went anywhere or had more than a few friends, but we did care for each other despite the unspoken understanding that there was little chance we would be together in the years to come. It was, in a way, sad that we felt that way. We felt that this whole thing would be temporary, yet afraid to initiate that fate. We lived in various places around the Virginia-Highlands neighborhood, living in rented rooms and apartments in the early eighties. Her son, Jimmy, spent much of that time in Richmond with his father but would be with us usually in the summer. In the summer of 1983, my relationship with Annie ended. After almost six years we were at the end of what we knew, from the beginning, would be an unlikely story. The difference of race and age might have been enough itself. As much as there were things about her soft and fun personality I loved, they could not withstand the pressure of her often erratic paranoid reactions and my real, if not suppressed, belief that I would never marry nor have children with her. I was not without fault; I got high often, didn't talk things out, and probably, was just immature. In July she moved back to California. She said she would go out and stay with her friend, Zelda, for a few months. Emotionally, we both felt it was the end, but we did not "declare" it, which, seemed to make it easier. I realized the day afterwards when Annie left that heartbreak is relative, that sometimes it is more sadness than heartache, the sadness of failure after a long commitment of time and emotion.

Remarkably, that same summer Birnur's relationship with her husband ended. She had moved into her own apartment, things changed. I had helped her move and we found ourselves alone together. That day, as they say, nature ran its course. After having developed a relationship that seemed to click on all levels, we now knew our lives should be together. I would visit her on my lunch break, sometimes at 2am or later, she would have something for me to eat quickly before our passions were served. We spent a couple months keeping it secret, realizing people would believe it had been the cause of the separations from our spouses, but those relationships had failed long before. And even though I began seeing her immediately after Annie left, the spilt was just a matter of time because it was a matter of real love that got my ass in gear to end it.

Later that year I moved to a dayside shift and began to cover all the everyday stories that make the news. I worked weekends and evenings, and by this time, my relationship with Birnur had become very strong and we considered moving in together. We took a trip to Florida in December and had a special time. The beach sunsets in the winter were beautiful. The following February, Annie returned from California. I told her about Birnur, the jealousy that had always been present, overwhelmed her rational side. Although she understood things were over between us, she was so enraged she did everything possible to show it. One evening I was at Mack's house with Birnur and Annie showed up. Mack wasn't home but she banged on and on at the door using some hard object, leaving imprints that remained for years. I tried to go out and calm her down, but her eyes were wild. She paced around and flailed her arms saying "where is she, where is she damnit?" In a careless moment, she slipped by me and ran into the front door pulling it closed behind her, and I did not have a key. I jumped from side to side for a second before turning and running for the side entrance to the kitchen, praying that it was unlocked. I could see the door and yet my thoughts were about the back of the house, in case I had to get in from there. I hit the handle and it turned, luckily. I ran to the back bedroom where Annie and Birnur were confronting each other from opposite corners, "come'on you bitch" Birnur said rather calmly. Annie was breathing heavily, her eyes wide and straining, with her fist clinched. I moved in front of her slowly persuading and forcing her out of the house.

It was stupid that I had caused such a dangerous moment, always trying to be nice, trying not to hurt feelings, trying to let Annie go softly. When I should have been unequivocal and direct with her, I was sentimental and tried to remain friendly. However, after those events, I was cutting all ties, giving her any of the mutual possessions we had, even the car. I saw Annie once or twice over the next ten years, at a store or some place we might pass each other, but we would speak just briefly and move on. I thought about her every now and then, not in any longing way, but just hoping she was ok. She was, after all, a big part of my young manhood, and my early years in Atlanta. I never saw or heard anything about her after the mid-nineties. She would be in her late sixties now. I hope she and Jimmy have been well.

It wasn't very long before Birnur and I lived together. Initially, I moved in with her and her roomate, Rengin, another young woman from Turkey. The three of us shared the two bedroom apartment for about a year and a half. We would joke that we were like a very popular television series in the early eighties; 'Three's Company.' We were all close like family and would refer to her, jokingly, as our daughter. Rengin has remained our closest friend for over thirty years. She moved back to Turkey in 1987, married and had a son, but we remained like family and visited her as much as Birnur's real family in Turkey. Birnur, herself, would have had to return in 1985 because of her visa status but I couldn't let that happen. We had been together for about two years and the only way she could stay in the states would require we get married. We briefly thought about her leaving . . . for a few seconds. Her divorce was done and now it was a matter of how we would tie the knot.

Birnur is not religious, in fact an atheist, and had no desire for a big "church wedding" or any big wedding for that matter. In Turkey, many people are married in a civil ceremony as a legal function, with family and close friends of course, but not necessarily the kind of "event" we think of here. Yes, there are grand spectacles held for some, usually the wealthy indulging themselves, or in smaller villages that celebrate as a community. But in most cities with the educated class, it is not usually as glamorous as in the west. Birnur was very progressive and had no compunction about just going down to the courthouse and seeing the judge. "I don't need a judge or priest to give me permission to be with the man I love" she has always said, and was only compelled because it was the only way she could stay. I think deep down she felt different, but Birnur has always been very pragmatic and independent. "I just don't want to get married on my lunch break" I told her, as we talked about our plan.

We had been living in a small rented house for a couple months and thought we would just get married in the backyard. Valerie helped us plan a small, simple but charming wedding less than two weeks later on April 20, 1985. My mom came down from Richmond, Maynard was my best man, Rengin the maid of honor, and mostly coworkers or Turkish friends were there on a very pretty and warm day. Birnur was beautiful. So petite and delicate, with an off-white, lace trimmed dress, hair pulled up with baby's breath tucked sweetly on one side, she was every bit a princess. I was in an off-white tuxedo, about as '80's as you can get. My cousin, Cleo Lacy, a reverend from Griffin, Georgia, read the vows we repeated. Birnur had asked him not to mention God, per se, but he slipped it in as any good preacher would. It was not an issue; our eyes were locked on each other every minute, with unbroken smiles. We were totally tickled with ourselves, laughing through cake and champagne, flaunting our happiness. We flew to New York for our honeymoon, walking all day venturing into cafés and visiting landmarks. Chinatown lured us with whole roasted duck sold from windows and we would sit on the riverside with greasy fingers and cold beers, never losing our grin since the wedding. Little moments like that defined our time there, just being casual New Yorkers. It was something we did each of the next few years, although trips to the beach, New Orleans, the mountains, a cruise, and trips to Turkey also filled those years before children. But, New York holds special memories of our early days as husband and wife.

At the time, I did not reflect so much on the notion that, as conglomerated as my identity was, I would be now, as the saying goes, one with a Turk. It almost seems poetic. When I was young my older brothers and sisters would say jokingly that I should marry a white woman because it would be easier. However, I would not marry a white woman or a black woman. I would marry outside both, in a way, just like me.

With both of us working at Channel 11, we commuted together and had the same shift for a few years. She became an assignment editor, the person who sets up stories and assigns crews to cover them, as well as listens to the six or seven scanners for any breaking news. We worked together as closely as any couple, and then went home together. They were fun years. When you're young and happy, it can only be fun. The story of the next thirty years of marriage, two children, Melody and Orman, and the many, many stories of laughter, pride, happiness, in struggle and pain, I will leave to other memoirs for family. I probably have as much on video as in my memory. It should certainly playback priceless times for them in their future. All else withstanding, Fatherhood rings deeply in my identity.

"Youngblood," was a DJ on WCLK radio Saturday mornings, playing old soul music and entertaining listeners with a unique gravelly voice and knowledge of "old school" culture. Youngblood, and his music, were the soundtrack for me on the weekend mornings I worked for almost seven years. Over those years, I would find myself covering the same annual events, and the same recreational stories that happen on the weekend. A 'Run' for this cause or another, a Frisbee or horseshoe contest, park events and fairs, air shows and dog shows. Weekends spent watching people enjoy their lives, which in turn, was enjoyable for me. Unfortunately, I could also count on being around tragedies. Crime, accidents, fires, and drownings, required I watch as people endured some of the worst days of their lives. The photographers and reporters that work those stories, whether tragic or comic, all knew each other. Like police officers and paramedics, the media all found themselves at the same places all the time, and naturally, we were all friends to some extent. While competitive in getting a special piece of video or sound, most time was spent sharing a laugh or complaining about our stations' operations. There is an old saying, "hurry up and wait," which defined what we did so often. "Such 'n such is having a press conference," or, "he should be leaving the courthouse now . . . go, go!" We'd rush to assignments only to end up waiting for long periods. Never far from our cameras, we would inevitably strike friendships. The familiar faces at news events might also be politicians or police, usually part of what we covered, but not necessarily "the story." They understood our jobs and we understood theirs, so the relationships were a bit more casual than it would be with the general public. It was not unusual to become friends with them as well, perhaps not socializing together, but well-acquainted enough to trust one another.

At crime scenes or horrible accidents, you might see the media or police grinning or smiling at each other carrying on a mundane conversation. It's not because they are calloused or insensitive to what had happened, but what had happened had been seen often by us. But the work could never be predictable, and sometimes the pain was difficult to shield, especially when children were involved. After years of fatal shootings and wrecks, fires and sometimes bizarre deaths, the scene could be processed sometimes nonchalantly. However, when I had to do a piece at the children's hospital where little five-year-old Johnny needs a new heart, and you're in the room with tearful parents and grandparents at his bedside, holding still the wall of water over your eyes, as you look into the viewfinder, was never easy. Colleagues and other professionals who were working could help, but few things could alleviate the emotional pressure of the room.

One Saturday afternoon, I went to cover the drowning of a young boy about seven, in an apartment complex swimming pool. I arrived at the lower middle-class complex and could see the ambulance and police at the end of the parking lot adjacent to the pool. It appeared to be a small pool with young boys and girls moving around in a type of slow motion. There weren't any news people, only the ambulance and a single police car. I unloaded my gear and prepared for the scene of distraught and crying adults and bewildered children. I had to park about fifty yards away and I checked my battery levels and audio settings on my camera as I started to walk. After just a few steps, I recognized the jingle of keys and cuffs and the hard sole shoes of an officer behind me. I didn't turn, expecting him to catch up with me in just a few moments and, as usual, ask me to be respectful and keep back a certain distance. I had no doubt he would be friendly, as we were both doing our jobs, and I knew the routine.

The bounce of the belt and keys reached my side and I turned and glanced at him. He was a county deputy, but from another county, I later realized. "A kid drowned it seems" I said, and then sighed with a slow negative nod. He mumbled something and I looked at him again. His eyes were staring straight ahead, like a blind man, eyes open but seeing nothing, with his mouth barely closed. Sometimes, cops can be stoic and not say much, a kind of tough guy here on business demeanor, so I just continued to ready my camera. I figured he was going to play that role and there wouldn't be any small talk or information. Again, he mumbled something I did not hear and I looked at him closely. This time, I saw it, I saw his eyes slope and strain, then he said it again several times, "It's my son, it's my son . . . it's my son." Even today, I cry as I write this. I was stunned, almost coming to a stop, saying something reflexive like "oh my God, God, I'm so sorry." I was so taken off guard I just looked at him, oblivious to the next few steps as if I was being carried. He was silent, but had the involuntary jerks of breath you might see in a child that is trying to stop crying.

I did not know what to say or what to do. What do you say? This deputy, like many in his job and many in mine, was used to handling the unpredictable reactions of grieving relatives, but now, was upside down in a familiar yet unimaginable place. We walked together for a few yards with my head spinning, not knowing how to respond, not only to him but also at him from a journalistic approach. We all have seen the images of a grieving parent or relative where the cameraman gets in close and asks the dumb ass question, something I had never done nor would ever do, but I had to include him. It was part of the story that the boy's father was a deputy. He walked ahead of me, walking with what might have appeared as intent authority from a distance, while I could only think, "damn . . . fuck." At the scene, I could hear the whispers of kids and some adults, "das his daddy, aawh, he a police man too"— "girl das so sad . . ." I stayed back and tried to save him at least the aggravation of a camera in his face. I did what was necessary to inform about the situation, but not the gratuitous display of suffering. He managed to hold it together while family, and other officers, tried to console him. It was rare to see an officer grieving so deeply, and it was difficult for those working that day to see a colleague in that situation. We all would second think our duties, but still perform them.

Some of my colleagues would have no problems getting real close in a case like that or chasing after a mother with her face in her hands. They would say, "You have to do your job, not be so sensitive, the public has a right to know." All that bullshit you hear from producers, and some in the field, trying to paint themselves as strong journalists, as oppose to "good TV" farmers reaping their favorite crop . . . shock. That was their job, which was and is the edict. Controlling the influence of sympathy at scenes like a drowning, or any tragedy, is required sometimes as a journalist, but to consciously deny basic empathy is unfaithful to the purpose of journalism. We cannot deny our humanity any more than that deputy in uniform could deny his that day.

Say it loud! . . . 1976.

The 'fro' in the wind slowed me down,
or perhaps I was just the wrong color . . .

Mother's Day 1976, the siblings; from left, Vicki, Ruth, Chuck, Butch, Valerie, Monte, and the two youngest, Rick and Robert.

My brother Chuck with supporters shortly after his historic Richmond city council win in 1977. Our new brother in law, Maynard Jackson, is second from right.

April 20, 1985. Maynard was my best man,
Rengin Nalbantoglu was Birnur's maid of honor.

My sister, Valerie, and her husband,
the late great mayor of Atlanta, Maynard Jackson.

On the job, somewhere, sometime, in the early nineties.

Two clowns with reporter Simeon Smith.

Birnur, 1987.

The best of times, my kids, Melody and Orman on vacation in Florida.

Nine

Good TV, good radio, that's the product. We were told we had to be good storytellers, that we should make each event or activity a compelling mix of words and images. Good story telling is as human and purposeful as gathering food, or even, gathering "news." That is understandable and smart, but too often it becomes priority. Often, the broadcasting of 9-1-1 calls serve no purpose but to sensationalize delivery. Facts are never contradicted by an image or sound, just juiced up for consumption. How often do we see things that have nothing to do with news, traditional definition withstanding, but simply an array of human-interest stories . . . the endless quest for the next "Man Bites Dog" allure. The information that we need to help understand why things are as they are is difficult and time consuming to produce. It may be a public service, but it doesn't sell the product of private interests. After all, we have to compete with the commercial world, honest entertainment like "Youngblood."

The early signs of what TV news would become, that being less news, came in the fashion of producers who were, by their own pronouncement, TV producers not "news" producers. "I'm not a news producer, I'm a television producer, I'm making good television" boasted Kerry, a weekend producer in the late eighties. The morning meeting of photographers, reporters, and video editors were a bit incredulous, but by now, had heard this version of our new menu for "the customers" from management. Kerry, and many with his approach, went on to high places in Gannett, the channel 11 parent company, becoming "news" directors or managers in corporate positions. In the local markets, the last decades have seen waves of pretentious "mission statements," new looks, new anchors, new technology and styles. Every station has tried to find a formula to draw, and keep viewers. Ironically, they all ultimately look exactly the same. No matter where in the country you travel, the local news will be the same, the same music, the same announcers, the sets, the slogans, the formats, all the same. With fewer and fewer owners consolidating the operations, a template, not unlike a fast food chain, is set for all. The independent lunch business does not exist on the main thoroughfares of any large American town, only the same familiar nine or ten franchise giants, creating an indistinguishable landscape. If you did not know where you were, you would not know where you are. The same could be said of the news landscape.

The emphasis on good television meant live broadcast with visual, animated motion as the priority. It wasn't that we didn't report important news, but it was rarely "covered." The things that we covered, meaning cameras and live shots, teases before a commercial break, and the general promotion of the story were, with the exception of crimes or accidents, the things that made good TV. All the elements of what made primetime popular would be the criteria that dictated what went into the show. The phrase "if it bleeds it leads" would be a popular description, first used by journalists to characterize the style of local news. Many reporters were asked to do sometimes silly, even risky stunts to enhance this priority, whether drama, comedy, rage, suspense, or just bizarreness, it was prime-time at six o'clock. I recall back in my very early days in 1981 or so, when it was decided to send a crew with a black technician to a Klan rally in Stone Mountain. It was not so much intentional to provoke the Klan, more the decision not to replace him as a crew member just to appease them. We knew how the attendees would react, as they had in the past, with shouts and looking outraged. No one expected any violence, it would be hard to imagine something done in full view of several cameras, even from the morons in the Klan, but it was still, in a sense, "baiting" the Klan, not observing. I have mixed views about this because it is good to expose those pathetic idiots, but at the time I believed the intent was more selfish.

It was a form of staging that would get more and more sophisticated, on both sides of the camera, over the next couple of decades. Shakespeare said "All the world's a stage." Indeed, today he might say "All the world is staged."

Today, everyone has seen the play so often they know all the roles and act accordingly when it is their turn on camera. That kind of expected "action," if you will, makes it easy to create the good TV that keeps the eye's attention. As technology permitted more and more stories, it became apparent to me, whatever we covered, legitimate things of importance or the water skiing squirrel, it was all just an excuse to do "TV." Often over the years, people trying to get their cause or business or event covered by TV would approach me asking how to get coverage. I let them know the best way was to come up with a visual gimmick, an event that would bait the cameras. Once the cameras are there, you have the opportunity to emphasize the reason.

One day in the early nineties, in a meeting for our noon newscast, one developing story was the legal battle going on between lawyers for the King center, Rosa Parks, and Boston University. I wasn't literally present but it was the talk of the newsroom that day. At issue was the possession of private notes and writings of Dr. King. Rosa Parks believed some of them belonged to her, which the King center argued against, as well as Boston University. It was, as they say, a boring story that requires the reporter to make chicken salad from chicken shit. "People don't care, this has no visual element at all" said someone at the table. "No, this is historical stuff that people want to see, here in Atlanta" said another. After a few minutes, they decided to do a "reader," a few seconds of information read to the camera by an anchor. A few moments after that, the lead producer for the noon show, a young twenty-something blonde with rosy cheeks and a perky smile, asked a question, somewhat to herself but also to everyone, "who is Rosa Parks, anyway?" The table fell silent for a second as a dozen eyes blinked and bounced. This producer was a hard working young woman that wanted to do a good job, but she was emblematic of the reason so many Americans are poorly informed. She had been hired to produce a television newscast in Atlanta, not Topeka, not in Butte, not Miami, but Atlanta, Georgia. She was tasked with discerning which events, and what information was important to folks in Atlanta, home of the civil rights movement and the so-called Black Mecca. Yet, this young woman did not know who Rosa Parks was. The genuine lack of historical perspective was not and generally is not a problem for television producers, particularly on the local level. It would not be a criterion necessary for good television. Granted, virtually everyone in the newsroom knew about Rosa Parks, but it was hard not to shake one's head.

It was a glimpse of the new trend, waves of young producers whose concern was as much the contour of a show as the content. That concept allowed managers to construct not just a new mousetrap, but to redefine the mouse. With new prey, so to speak, you bring flare at the expense of facts, entertainment in lieu of information, begetting the notorious infotainment. We once had a reporter pretend to be an airline pilot, (this was pre Sept. 11) uniform and all—by the way a federal crime—to see how far through security he could get, even on the tarmac. Another time we had a crew drive through a typical suburban neighborhood with a remote control garage door opener to see how many doors they might open. Yes, it was a striking demonstration that proved a point; how vulnerable remote openers can leave you. The manner of that demonstration, however, was highly irresponsible. Would alarm systems go off, were there pets, or even children in the garage that might run out, wasn't this illegal entry? In each of these examples there were people in the newsroom who were opposed to the way it was done. There are many good journalists, and good people, who are trying each day to do the best they can for the public. However, they typically are not running the stations. Those directing the focus of an operation or the style of the station, or network, have but one quest, not so much to keep the public informed, just to keep them watching . . . "so, Carol, show us whats behind garage door number three!" That is not to say if they believed good journalism would be profitable they would not do it, but they are competing with the medium itself.

Today, the local newscast in large part, if not covering the weather or crime, seems to be morphing into some sort of "social site." Filled with YouTube videos and what's "trending" on the web, they invite us to share pictures and opinions, while anchors add their "comments" to virtually every story. They've been forced by this deafening digital menu to join what they cannot beat; Facebookers eager to be "liked." Older journalists, especially in print but also in TV and radio, are being moved out systematically. Decades of dedicated service mean little when the objectives change. Journalism has been on a slippery slope with television for decades as well, and now it is but a passenger on digital super rail. With cell phones everywhere, shocking, salacious, amazing, funny videos are a constant menu. Who needs journalists; we have encyclopedias and cameras in our pocket. As author and media critic Neil Postman said years ago, we will be "amused to death." A medium that keeps us so amused until we find ourselves unwittingly bemused.

Many of us realized that the corporate hunger for profit from the news divisions would not only affect our salaries and job definitions but the public interests as well. The request, in fact demand, from the government that television networks provide a certain amount of public service in exchange for the use of air frequencies, would be glossed over with a pretense of that service. The separation or firewall from the corporate interests would come down like a controlled demolition. News, as we see, is on all day, 24hrs. The cost involved in producing "The Beverly Hillbillies" to generate revenue is far more than sending a cameraman to weather stricken Iowa or to loom over acrimonious politicians. Don Hewitt of CBS once said, "We need to make interesting what is important." Well, there is no doubt that now the motto in the business is "We need to make important what is interesting." In the nineties, the media totally danced around the governments tune denying the admitted fact, albeit a few years later, that the CIA was allowing, and in essence facilitating, the crack epidemic in the black communities of LA and other large cities in the 1980s to finance the Contras in Nicaragua. Ostracizing and defaming the journalist that broke the story to the point of his suicide. That was about Ronald Reagan's boys. It broke, however, at a time when a Clinton girl named Monica shocked America about the things presidents lie about. The CIA selling crack? Nah, let's go with the blow job in the oval office.

For a few years it was just that simple, give them good TV, however, as news became an obvious commodity, good TV was not good enough. Rupert Murdoch took it the next step with FOX News. If the idea was to sell, you have to provide a product they want; show and tell them what they want to hear, and believe. Murdock realized there was a large segment of America that grew weary of the social changes, tired of seeing the country trying to live up to its principles. They wanted the old narrative, and they wanted it justified. It proved successful. Now, other media venues are catering to groups outside the "foxhole," whether to liberal progressives, or "pop-minded" young people, fashioning a product to specific interests. The problem is that we are developing such calcified narratives on everything, from race to religion, from history to health, walls go up. Even when a certain event or truth is realized, it is conveyed with the lexis of that narrative.

That becomes such a problem especially with politics, which makes it a problem with our problems. When the intent is to keep the audience, regardless of what's in its best interest, then the focus is to keep the horse race or prize fight a constant. And then, the quest of media is to not challenge or adjudicate statements but simply to turn to the opponent and await his swing, not to point out if the swing is a foul because they have to be "balanced" between the fighters. "So, Mr. Wilson, the senator says the world is flat, what is your argument against that? We want to give you equal time." That posture, where both sides have equal validity and deserve equal weight, structurally serves the side that is more willing to mislead or cheat. TV news has been, in my mind, one reason we have become so unaware in general of the issues and truths that put us where we are. Information is certainly available and to an extent, almost overwhelming, requiring a discerning eye. However, if your source is the typical evening network news, which is the case for most, you're getting the product of marketing and politics. This has made us the most docile, easily sold to society on earth, whether it's the latest drug, the reason for war, or an unthinkable reality show hothead for president.

The ubiquitous presence of "reality shows" is the result of how TV news took real events and real conflict and gave it, some would argue, entertainment value. The headline would not be, "Five shot at a local restaurant," but rather, "Terror at the Tavern!" or "Unhappy Hour." Promotion of "real-life" proved to draw viewers, and with cheap technology available independent producers saw as well its relatively low cost. While the majority of things on the newscast were the normal reports of events everyone is used to, special series were usually meant to feed the beast, show business.

Probably one of the best examples of the show business was the O.J Simpson trial, an endless wall-to-wall coverage of one crime. It was everything TV could ask for: vicious violence, the blond sex symbol, the black Mandingo ravishing her, drugs, fame, and the fallen idol. All live. It was, in a way, the last great lynching of the twentieth century. Not that Simpson was innocent, innocence or guilt was rarely the point with lynchings, the spectacle of black masculinity and its destruction, that historical context in the American psyche, black and white, was the essence of the attraction. The endless coverage from the slow speed chase to the verdict and beyond fed us all. And yet, the reaction to the verdict by many black people was mind-boggling to most whites. They saw what they believed to be celebrations of, in a sense, these murders. It was not that. What it was mostly was the notion that America had tasted a spoon of its own medicine. No one celebrated the idea someone got away with two brutal murders, but there was a catharsis a hundred years in the making. Again, black people were not so much happy that OJ got off, even believing in his innocence, as they were able to see the shoe on the other foot, finally, as the whole world watched. Maybe O.J did it, I don't know, some say there was drug cartel involvement. But the abject shock across white America was easily understood by blacks.

It was a manifestation, while perhaps ugly or startling on the surface, of being able to say to white folk "yeah, doesn't feel so good does it, that's fucked up, ain't it? imagine a lifetime of that feeling." The reasonable doubt the jury found was a product of history, the history of the LAPD, of the racist officers involved in the investigations. It was not inconceivable that evidence or crime scenes were manipulated. Johnny Cochran, OJ's attorney, had seen years of the kind of thing we see in police videos today, hardly news to black people then or now. He and his colleagues demonstrated reasonable doubt, beyond the glove that "doesn't fit, you must acquit." Most wanted to blame the mostly black jury, a set of peers denied countless black defendants—if a jury at all. It was just so much deeper than a single verdict about a contentious trial; it was all of us on trial, and we all tuned in.

A couple of years later, I actually had dinner with Johnny Cochran at his apartment home in New York City. His daughter, Tiffany, had been hired as a reporter and we worked together often. We had gone to New York to cover the anniversary of the "Million Man March," and had dinner one evening with him and his wife. We talked about the case a little but also about Maynard and civil rights history and mundane things as well. He was a charming and very smart guy, the type you would want to defend you. As well, I've met his client. I actually worked with OJ a couple of times in Barcelona at the 1992 Olympics. He was as nice as any of the TV personalities at NBC at the time. Who knew?

I remember we did a hidden camera series on the public works department of Atlanta. The idea was to show city employees on various job sites, doing or not doing work, pointing out the waste of tax dollars. Creatively titled "Men at Work," the "investigation" took several weeks, following crews to their job location and secretly videotaping their day. The video shown was, of course, scenes of lazy men leaning on shovels or standing around, some even asleep in their vehicles. One was even seen purchasing alcohol, though not consuming it, while on the job, and another urinating on a job site. While the video could not be disputed, it was the lack of journalism that became an issue for many in Atlanta. The five-part series was simply a video log of activity observed from a distance in an undercover van. The problem was there was no confirmation of men simply being "lazy." Were there reasons . . . waiting on equipment or parts, sleeping perhaps on lunch break, trainees or additional workers waiting to perform specific tasks during the job? There may have been legitimate reasons, however unlikely, but that prudent step to "check your sources" was not taken. Only after an uproar from civic and political leaders did we send reporters to question department heads and job supervisors to address, if not explain, the images in the videos. To the producers and mangers at the station, it was not necessary in the body of the original stories. The video spoke for itself, period.

A week-long series with no reference or comparison to other municipalities or counties in the suburbs, which just happened to be white, it left many angered. Only after the outcry did we send cameras to observe other workers who were, by which time, certainly cognizant of the attention. This is exactly the point about giving the customer what he wants. The "customer" in this case was our identified viewer base, thirty-five to fifty-four-year-old white Georgia males. Although I doubt anyone actually said it openly, the appeal of images that supported that historical, racist portrayal was not lost on anyone. It may as well have been called "Boys at Work."

In the early eighties I covered the Georgia legislature at the state capitol. In the lower floor of the capitol building there were rooms that held old records and documents that were introduced from sessions going back over seventy years. It was amazing to read some of the bills introduced in 1957. Not all were passed, but the agenda of those representatives in the years following 'Brown vs. Board of Education' and other civil rights laws was razor sharp. These were proposed laws that forbade blacks and whites from even walking together. It was amazing, almost unbelievable to see some of those bills that actually made it out of the committee. In that same room one day I came across an old dictionary. It was large and heavy and had obviously been used by members and staff in decades past. It was published in 1912, with ornate and fancy calligraphy in its opening pages. I thumbed through it to kill time one day and just happened to come across the word 'connive' or 'conniving.' As an example or demonstration of that meaning, was written the phrase "nigger in a wood pile." I said to myself wow, a clear official example of how black men were perceived. Today a lot has changed, but for many still, a black man is suspicious by definition.

Sometimes the real world is so difficult to believe, much less understand, that the task of discerning cause and effect can seem hopeless. The fundamental questions of good and evil, normal or crazy, are always at the core of almost any story. Many times, stories would take an offbeat turn. Once, we were following police on a seatbelt check when they stopped a young woman. She had her young son, about three, in the back seat, neither she nor the child was buckled. There was even a child seat next to him. The mother was only going a few blocks to the convenience store so she thought it was ok. She even said on camera "I didn't buckle myself either, because I said if something happened it was gonna happen to me too." All of us were baffled at the mentality, including the officer. But it went further; she was going to the store, again said on camera, to buy lottery tickets. This woman believed she could win the lottery but would not be in an accident. That can almost seem like "normal" behavior for human beings, denying overt odds on a "belief" basis. Whether a political issue or a warehouse fire, we seem to measure events against some pretense of 'normal' or 'good.' Pretense because there are always double, or even triple, standards applied to the coverage of events, depending on what has happened to whom. Homicides are probably one of the more glaring examples. The murder of a young white woman vs. a young black man is an easy example—white woman: good, shouldn't happen—black man: bad, probably had it coming.

I remember the deaths of an elderly black couple that happened on Sunset Ave. It was near the home Martin Luther King Jr. lived in early in the sixties. It was a short mention on the weekend news, no profiles of the couple, no real pressing of police about it, just an unfortunate event in the hood, attributed to perhaps a crazed crackhead. It was something that stuck with me for years. I wondered what their lives had been about. I learned their names and that they had been married almost fifty years, but the crime scene I saw that early Saturday morning after their murders had me imagining their whole lives.

I had gone to get what we call a "real-estate shot" of the address where it happened. There wasn't any police activity so we would simply show the house and anything that indicated police or medical involvement. It was a cool fall morning with a bright sun that had raised just above the roof of the small simple house. It was not unlike almost any home in sight, with needs that required money, however, kept as clean and tidy as an elderly man and woman might keep it. I noticed that only a single piece of yellow crime scene tape was flapping from a tree. Put up half-heartedly, it had fallen, leaving not much direction to the public. I started setting up my camera and noticed the front door practically half-open. After getting the outside pictures, I walked up to the door to glance in, curious more than thinking of shots for the story. I stepped in and I could not, nor want to, believe my eyes. The small living area with a couple of chairs, a TV, a small chest of drawers and a lamp was literally covered with blood. It was like an overdone horror film, blood strewn all across the walls, across the television, the floor, even pools of it in the seat of the chairs. After catching my breath, I tried to grasp the reality of what must have happened. The police had said they were beaten to death probably by a crackhead hunting for cash, and in my mind's eye, I could see that poor couple trying to escape. And in my mind, I could not escape, again, the random, delicate and unexplainable course of life.

That couple had likely endured many hardships and likely seen many triumphs, but how likely their lives should end like that. A soldier survives war only to die a week before or after his return home. A couple lives through decades in a society indifferent to their happiness, and yet, is killed by one in their own community, perhaps a child they had once knew and extended kindness. But even these sad deaths, were treated with a casualness that upset me. The home was left literally abandoned by the police, left for the neighborhood to explore on a sunny Saturday afternoon. The casual approach we, the media, took simply because of where it happened, was all too typical. It was just a pitiful case of a pitiful neighborhood, all but forgotten by the next weekend. It didn't happen where it wasn't supposed to happen, so it was just a sad thirty seconds on the evening news.

The sad reality is that society makes the same kind of 'auto-assessment.' When crime happens to black people we 'understand.' It speaks to the notion of a perception over a hundred years old. That perception is clear from Florida to Utah to New Jersey, derived from information and portrayals we receive in the media, our cultural common denominator. Whether in Utah or New Jersey, rich, poor, or Jehovah Witness, we draw from the same well. Virtually any image or portrait we paint in our minds about any people on earth is, by and large, from what we've seen on TV or movies. Whether Chinese or Gay or Muslim or Mexican or Black or corporate for that matter, we know in our minds from what we have seen on TV. When George Zimmerman was acquitted by a jury for the killing of Trayvon Martin, it was because the jury was empathetic. Empathy that served the officer who shot down the young man on the streets of Ferguson, Missouri, or the officer who choked to death a black man on the streets of New York, the examples go on and on. The juries and investigators understood the threat, empathy by virtue of that common denominator, decades long reinforcement on television and movies, endless images on their local news about black crime, the all too often security camera videos of a black male killing a convenience store clerk, or the body bags of gang violence.

While white folk may have fled the cities, most TV stations remained in town. Crime happened out in the suburbs and country, but crime in the city was close and easy because, like anywhere, population and poverty allow much to cover. So, it seemed anytime you saw non-celebrity black folk on TV, they were criminals. Hence, it's easy to understand why Zimmerman suspected and followed Trayvon, why he feared for his life when the hooded black male confronted him. Who couldn't empathize with that?

Video, however, is now showing the other side; we are becoming aware of what can result from such stereotypes. Today, a dozen years after 9/11, it seems even with that empathy we are taken aback by some of the blatant actions by police. There has been a trickle down of the Bush doctrine: pre-emptive strike with overwhelming force. Police are being militarized and trained to "engage immediately" the slightest "perception" of threat. With black men, the perception seems solid, thus engagement. We all know the majority of police are brave, well-meaning officers. That should not be understated. But now, the almost weekly videos of the pre-emptive or overwhelming force, has us realizing a little empathy for the black man himself. Change comes from action, action comes from attention. The amount and type of attention usually portends the change, or not. But an interesting dynamic is changing things. With a cell phone "witness," the attention proliferates instantly. Martin Luther King said, "An injustice anywhere is a threat to justice everywhere." Now, an injustice anywhere is everywhere virtually in real time. It will be fascinating for future historians to study the shift in response to events given this new mode of attention.

Ten

The legitimate side of the coin, which gave us incredible TV, was "breaking news," the big magnet of dramatic events seen live as they unfold. The high-speed chase, or any speed chase for that matter, is probably the most familiar, but there are hostage situations, fire rescues, and other dramatic scenes for the cameras. The responsibility of journalists in those cases is hard to delineate, usually holding back on the coverage only if it put people in direct danger. The question of showing the possible harm or even death of someone on live television is a very tight rope to walk. That very aspect is the reality behind the appeal, sadly. The bottom line is simple; this is a business that competes for attention, and like a flamboyant peacock, sometimes demands it.

One of those cases was in the early nineties. A Delta flight coming from Europe was having problems with its landing gear. The crew could not confirm, through their instruments, if the wheels were down so a fighter jet was sent to visually determine it. The gear was down; however, whether they were locked and stable was anyone's guess. For over an hour, the plane flew to burn off gas and prepared to land. In the newsrooms around the city, and the networks as well, managers debated whether to show the landing "live." The possibility of the gear collapsing and the scene of a skidding, and likely, flaming crash landing, put journalists in a corner. Do we exploit the live images that would have everybody glued, or consider we'd be subjecting family and friends, who by now were well aware of the situation, to the horror of viewing the violent death of their loved ones as it happened? Again, the weight of journalism could not usurp the issue of TV competition. The conscious decision to broadcast live a very possible outcome of mass death, is pathetic. Why not show executions? Ratings would be huge. I have no doubt, today the event would be a 'no-brainer' . . . show it. In my mind, it was not justified. Thankfully, it was a smooth landing. This approach is very normal now. Information has to be delivered in an audio-visual format or it is almost illegitimate. It's been a progression over decades, but nonetheless, where we are. They say "monkey see, monkey do," and we find ourselves where monkey "must see" or monkey will not know what to do.

The subject of death and suffering is unavoidable for a news cameraman. The observance of, at times absorbed, tragedy can take a toll. Seeing someone die is not forgotten, whether in a war zone or high-rise fire, the image takes on a hard to explain memory. One is usually in a high stress situation, maneuvering around police or fire fighters, watching each step and keeping a kind of 360-degree radar, for not only your safety, but to capture the relevant pictures that are needed. One event I witnessed was especially difficult because it seemed so hard to believe the victim could not be rescued. It was early June of 1989, I had just returned from a blistering hot Las Vegas, covering the Southern Baptist Convention. It was the beginning of just another early summer day, expecting a routine press conference or some show at the convention center. An intern was tagging along with me that day and early on there was a fire call on Peachtree Street, less than a minute away. We jumped in the car and soon saw the smoke pouring out of several windows in a mid-size high-rise. I pulled into a parking lot next to the building and we could see people leaning from a smoking window. I hopped out, grabbed my camera, and told the intern to hang back and try to gather information from witnesses or fire officials.

As I walked toward it, I prepared the proper settings on my camera and, from the corner of my eye, I saw an object drop from the building. Within seconds, I was just feet from a woman who had jumped. She was moving, and had miraculously survived. EMS responders immediately surrounded her and I looked up about seven or eight floors above to see five other people at the busted glass window she had been leaning from. They were screaming, but tried to remain calm while the hot black smoke poured over their heads out of the building. I pointed my camera at them, zoomed in, and saw their frightened, yet patient eyes waiting for help. One man and four women squeezed into a window frame of maybe 4'x5' edged with sharp broken glass. Their faces blackened, with hair and clothes in every twisted shape possible.

Fire trucks could be heard screaming blocks away while onlookers gathered on the sidewalk across the street. Firefighters ran urgently with hoses and oxygen tanks in and around the building. I spent a few minutes with my camera on the people in the window, trying to say to them, through my viewfinder, "don't jump, they will be there soon," while glancing away every few seconds to what was being done and wondering how I should handle the shot of one of them falling or jumping. Should I scream for them to hold on, should I follow them falling with the camera? My heart was pounding. The building had others at several broken out windows, but the group I was watching was in the most eminent danger. With a third alarm sounded, other ladder trucks were arriving and began rescue attempts. From Peachtree Street, they began stretching the long ladders almost horizontally to the sixth floor. The fire started when an electrician was changing a high voltage fuse that arched and flashed fire, the intense heat and smoke leaving impossible the escape routes for office workers at that end of the building as well as the entry to that area for firefighters. The only way to them was from outside until the heat and smoke could be knocked down inside.

Everyone who had been on the other floors was able to get out, but about twenty on the sixth were trapped. The electrician was killed, and many were in grave danger from smoke inhalation. Some of the radio transmission from the command post was on loudspeaker and we could hear the status of what was being done. Each rescue would have to be done across a ladder bridge, more of a crawl than stepping, and it seemed forever. Once ladders reached the people above me, I moved around back where people were yelling about others at another window. I looked up and saw two black men leaning on the window ledge; one was holding the other in his lap with his hand under his chin trying to keep his head up toward open air. The smoke was not as bad as the other window but still it was apparent how distressed they were. The man being held was heaving for breath every few seconds and the other tried to keep him close to the fresh air, while he himself was now hardly able to keep his eyes open from the heat and smoke.

By now, many photographers, including my co-workers, were on the scene. The fire fighters knew of these men but were unable to get to them. The heat and smoke on that floor was so intense they could not reach them from inside, and due to the design of the building they could not extend a ladder. The building had a very bad layout. Built partially over a parking deck that extended in the rear, access was very poor. The problem was the ladder truck could not get around back to a point they could extend to anyone in a window. Even if the trucks could get around, the top of the parking deck was the only space to stage the trucks, and the top floor of the deck was not built to support heavy vehicles, just an outdoor space for lunch tables, etc. People were running around screaming at firefighters and looking for a way to the window. It seemed the firefighters were preoccupied with others inside and simply had their hands full, or were forced to wait for the right apparatus to reach them.

Meanwhile, I'm seeing these two guys in the window just suffering, every minute or so shifting and leaning for air. The man being held closed his eyes and was in bad shape. I later learned, he had been rescued from the hallway by the man holding him and had already suffered a lot of smoke inhalation. His eyes would open now and then and look blankly into the sky. We all looked at each other like "God damn, what's the deal? Can't they get a helicopter and drop someone with a harness or from the roof with a rope, get one of those giant catch nets, something!" Ten minutes, fifteen minutes, these guys are still without any efforts that we could see to save them. I don't know why, and I don't think for a minute the fire department was not doing everything they thought possible, but I had to watch that man slowly stop his heaves for breath and eventually stop all movement. All I could say to myself, probably said it openly, was muh-tha-fuck! The fire fighters were finally able to reach them from inside and save the gentleman who had held his colleague for so long. Five died that day, more than forty hurt, in one of the worst fires in Atlanta in fifty years.

Many think Americans have become desensitized, from so much life and death on television, jaded simply by so much "been there done that" when it comes to what we have "viewed." There is a big difference when it is witnessed. When I see things on television today, whether good or bad, I can feel many times like I'm there. I can know what the photographer is doing and thinking, and by extension, sense the energy and feel of the event. This isn't to say news people are necessarily more empathetic or something, but to "witness" something can change you. To bear witness, or testify, is to have lived an event. There is a difference between the soldier who kills in battle and the soldier who kills with a drone from a video monitor, as one views and the other is witness.

What do you take away from seeing a man die in combat, or a fire like that? Of course, a deep sadness for the victims and families, but what was learned from it, and not in the sense of a careless technician or architect, but about empathy? In those twenty minutes, I went through every possible thought about what those men were going through, it is almost as if I had shared it in some ridiculous way. Does empathy grow in us after a first-hand experience, or are we born with varied degrees of it? The American Indians would say, "You have to walk a mile in a man's moccasins to know him." Is there a point where we become callous or hard and stoic after too much exposure? Maybe it's neither, maybe we just eventually realize that shit happens. Nevertheless, when it happens perhaps we are best prepared if we have learned, or gained, empathy. Maybe empathy can be a form of vaccine to bolster your understanding and fortitude, when shit happens to you.

———

The last seven or eight years in the business I actually spent helping people. I was producing and shooting a segment called 'Call for Action.' It was not so different from other ombudsmen at newspapers or TV stations, but it had a real "TV" aspect to it. We would make the "Call" on camera with a cell phone from the site or home of the problem. In the late nineties, cell phones had just become common and it had a real-time quality. That, and the reporter who made the calls, became very popular. Bill Liss, who had been in PR and was also a lawyer, had a way with words, in fact to the dismay of many, was never at a loss for them. But Bill was smart and savvy about the business world and knew how to intimidate, not just by threat of TV exposure, but his knowledge of the law. Bill also had one of those bigger than life personalities, sometimes he could be overbearing, and the person on the other end of that call found they were dealing with an irresistible force. At any rate, he got things done. The highlight of most of our stories was the phone call to the responsible party to fix the problem. Bill would raise his voice and demand they respond, gesticulating and demanding they take care of it; "like right now!" The thing that made it work was the fact that we would not name the person or company if they took action to fix things. This way there was opportunity to do the right thing before risking lots of bad exposure. Of course, there were cases so egregious the name or company would be front and center. Bill and I worked on behalf of old ladies, poor people, disabled folks and just ordinary people who had been denied fair treatment. We would also be involved with veterans, firefighters, children hospitals and many groups that deserved a little, or a lot, of help.

One story we worked on didn't help any person in particular, however it was really poignant. Often there would be 'calls' made for city or county government to clean an area or property that had become overwhelmed with trash or plant growth. In one such case, it involved an old graveyard at the back of a Black church on the east side of Atlanta. It seemed there had been a problem finding the current owner of the land; the church did not, oddly. We went by to interview a descendant whose great-grandfather had been buried there in the forties, and now could not locate his marker. The area was full of old ornate monuments and simple headstones weathered and broken, some dating back to pre-Civil War. We located it, after much searching, about fifty feet into the woods, totally overgrown. Bill made his trademark call to the county and soon the commission chairman was on the line.

After we did a little more taping, Bill left and I decided to explore the rest of the property that went back two hundred feet or so. As I noticed the headstones begin to end, ivy took over, covering the base of the trees and ground that was not so level, requiring I especially watch my step. After a few minutes, I turned to start back and saw a stone jutting up about a foot from the wide green leaves. I stepped pass it, almost ignoring it, but it caught my eye. There was something man-made or man-laid about it, like a giant arrowhead or perhaps a shark tooth. Looking closely, I remembered that slave graves were often dignified by a simple field stone, an unmarked marker. I grew anxious and began to look carefully around me, pushing back ivy from anything. I found another. I wasn't sure this could be an area slaves were buried but I didn't hesitate to take pictures and we followed up with the county.

A few days later the Dekalb county chairman, Bill, and myself were back at the graveyard. Stepping carefully through the brush, we found things that may have been markers or just a rock in the ground. But there was enough compelling about the two I found that the chairman decided to bring in a noted county historian. A few weeks later we found out, records were recovered indicating slaves had been buried at the back of the graveyard. It was not so unusual that it was done, but the historian, speaking to the entire county commission, revealed who owned them, and that at least one child was buried there with maybe eight or nine others. The original church at the site was White, its congregation long gone, but papers found through archive and family provided answers. Dekalb County decided to clear and maintain all the graves on the site, and recognize the small area in the back with more than just a rock.

Bill and I are proud of the work we did those days and remain good friends. There were more than several stories that made a wonderful difference in the life of someone. They were very rewarding. But there was something about helping a long lost soul, and the remembrance of those like him, that broaden that reward.

I guess one will believe I have become quite cynical about the news business . . . duh. To an extent perhaps, but I don't really blame the people I worked with; Lord knows I didn't study journalism in school. But the overriding issue is corporate interests. They will spend many millions on the Olympics or some disaster, but relatively nothing on issues that have proven to be of tremendous impact on the majority of Americans. TV gave me a front row seat to life, and in so much, a heck of a ride for almost thirty years. I know that I am lucky to say that, and I will always be grateful for the opportunity I was given. It is an amazing job to have when you can sit down with a homeless man living in the woods, in a cardboard box, and sit down with the president of the United States that same day. I did that.

Great places to live exist all over the world, but nowhere else can you find the range of people and possibilities here, good and bad. It is just that maybe my experience with a thing called deception has left me too sensitive to it. Deception, intentional or unintentional, creates such risk. I feel so disappointed with our inability or unwillingness to challenge deception even when looking clear-eyed at a naked emperor. I don't believe the upper echelons of management have some cold-hearted disregard for the public, I just believe they will not go, with any sustained attention, where it makes the public uncomfortable about our great narrative, especially in foreign policy. Around the world, especially now, it has become a joke: USA . . . U Stupid Americans.

OK, I've slammed the media enough.

———————

I believe we could do three things as a nation that would have real impact in the U.S., and consequently, much of the world. But none is possible without a fourth, the fourth estate or branch of government, a truly free and objective press, not the corporate masquerade. These three things may prove to be naïve or misconceived, but it's what I think. And what I think a lot of people think.

First, is campaign finance reform, or corruption reform you might say. Our dysfunctional and unresponsive congress is the result of a sea of cash. There has to be accountability to voters as well as donors. No one expects a politician, to an extent, to forget the hand that feeds him, it's been the game for millennium, but in the system as it is, the "little man" can truly forget any support that contradicts the agenda of "big business." A Princeton team of researchers concluded we are indeed an oligarchy, that the interests and cares of the majority of Americans play no role in policy. Only big business. Imagine if Teddy Roosevelt had said, "I speak with this big stick." That's what the Supreme Court is saying; the stick is speech. And it can be wielded in all manner to maintain policy which benefit the oligarchs. Why aren't we told who "sponsors" the politicians? Everything is sponsored, whether it's the name of a stadium, or the name of a city bus. It's so bad even the instant replay during televised games is being sold to a "Doritos" or "Bud Lite" sponsor. So, let's label the congress, no less money is spent on influence there. There has to be a constitutional amendment for public financing to free good politicians from the demand of cash that forces corruption.

When the army decides to use private security on its bases, yes, THE ARMY needs protection, you know something is rotten. Things like peeling potatoes or cleaning latrines, which was always done by soldiers, is contracted out to a crony of congressman Whoever. During Vietnam, only 1 in 20 personnel working in the armed forces were private contractors. By the mid-nineties, it was 1 in 6 and by the mid Iraq and Afghan wars greater than half the US personnel in those theaters were private groups cashing in on tax dollars, commanding millions. And our politicians are quite familiar with the unprecedented record profits being made. So, as much as we would like to "kick the bums out", it will take kicking the 'bucks' out of the game before we can get our representatives to represent the people.

Happily, for the "egolectuals" in the media, who sit around desk and analyze shit, they still win. If politicians are free to express their genuine positions, and hopefully that of their constituents, not just toting their corporate and partisan loyalties, there would still be plenty of mockery and acrimony to satisfy good TV. But I imagine corporate bottom-lines would fight hard to maintain the infinite campaign advertisement dollars the Supreme Court has given "voice." That voice, however, is simply used by politicians to finance the election industrial complex: consultants, pollsters, PACs, ad men, and the vast budgets needed for yes, you guessed it, TV. As CBS President Les Moonves said in 2012 "Super PACs may be bad for America, but they're very good for CBS," The 1996 Telecommunications Act has left CBS and five other corporate giants controlling over 90% of the media in this country, down from over 50 companies in the early eighties. So unfortunately, the status quo is in the interest of big media.

The last few election cycles brought more than a few clowns to the ring. All supportive of big money and corporate interests, but disguising it in a cloak of social issues: abortion, affirmative action, gays, gun rights etc., and the tough guy on national defense at all cost, including the constitution. The 2015-16 republican campaigns brought, mostly with Trump, very telling truths about the base of the party, although none a real surprise. The party has been on this trajectory since the early eighties when we began to hear about the "angry white male". The AM airwaves have been, and are, replete with talk shows serving his resentment, that anger that began 20 years earlier with a nasty liberal product called integration. Politicians too, but for many years there was at least, on its face, articulate expression, albeit full of dog whistles. But after the night the Negro was elected, the dogs would have no more of that. There would have to be an ever dumbing down of the message, if not the candidates themselves.

Since the likes of Tom DeLay and the Bush Congresses, the party has gerrymandered districts all over the country, contorting lines that allow the politician to pick his voters, assuring a republican victory. This was literally announced as the plan by Karl Rove in 2010. While votes for democrats outnumber Republicans nationally, they maintain an artificial majority in the congress by virtue of those prefabricated district wins. The senate has a republican majority yet they represent roughly ten million fewer people than the democrat and independent senators. And of course, a president that lost the popular vote.

I realize that many would argue there are real frustrations, real suffering in their world, legitimate reasons for the anger. There are real reasons they, and we, should be upset. The working class without a college degree is in the worst shape in modern memory. Technology is a big factor in this, but not the main problem. Corporate downsizing, outsourcing, union busting and wage freezing, all while doubling or even tripling the burden on the workforce, is familiar to all of us. The telling aspect to this is where the blame is attributed. Obama tries to initiate a jobs program to rebuild our crumbling bridges and roads, bring the minimum wage up, help with the ridiculous cost of college and they just say no. It's the Mexicans' fault, they keep those wages down.

In the first Republican debate of 2015, the newest clown in the room was indeed Donald Trump, the billionaire media court jester. Trump pointed out he had given lots to several of his opponents at some point for their campaigns or causes. While a couple pointed out they had not received his grace, if you will, another couple basically asked for some. "When I give them money they do what I want . . . That's a broke system," he insisted. He was testifying first-hand about the character of our corrupt system. "When I call them in a year or so they are there for me" he said, speaking generally about politicians. He, however, doesn't need the cash so he would answer only to "The Donald." It was a given; money is the boss. The issue of money in the game and the impact on policy and law was talked about only in the context of Trump's brief mention of it on stage, its entertainment value. The public, however, even in screams of tragic need, is simply observed like a homeless beggar, sad and powerless.

How is it that ninety percent of Americans want some sort of gun control: background checks, assault rifle bans, etc. Ninety percent saying do something please, yet nothing changes. Children from elementary classes to college campuses are gunned down and congress is content to do nothing. Nothing. Why? The answer put forth is "guns don't kill, people kill." In a sense it's absolutely true, even toddlers kill. But Americans have been taught from John Wayne to James Bond, and a million shows in between, that the way to resolve conflict, whether external or internal, is with violence, typically with a gun. It has become somewhat of a creed or ethos in America. Given that, why would we allow such ubiquitous opportunity for the violence? Is it so risky for congress to even appear to be limiting our right to bear what we want and when we want it? For many of us, we embrace the image of the strong independent cowboy, we believe in John Wayne. I think all of us defend the right to protect ourselves and property, but we don't need a Maserati to get from home to work; a Toyota will do fine. Most Americans can understand the thrill and the sport use of some of these weapons. If it was required that they be kept at a controlled and supervised club or shooting range, there would be no problem. But, this notion that 'John Wayne' can walk through a coffee shop with an AR-15 over his shoulder, because his state laws allow it; that is simply ridiculous. Why can't we get past this false creed of gun innocence? When President Obama said many Americans "cling" to their guns and religion, he hit a nerve. It was un-American to imply there was something wrong with that.

The success of the movie "American Sniper" is a good example. While it was based on a "true" story and a good movie per se, it was purposely absent of the whole truth in order to serve the narrative. Ironically, it would have been more 'Americanesque' had the story been of an underdog, outgunned, civilian sniper defending his homeland from an invading massive military power. As well, it just seems so un-American the concept of the sniper, to murder in cold blood an individual, much less a child, who has absolutely no defense at that moment. Even John Wayne wouldn't shoot a guy in the back. I can understand the argument about executing a loose killer, the imminent threat, carrying a bomb toward troops etc., but often as not, it was speculation. War is hell. But suffice it to say, our guy was killing savages. It would be helpful to see a sequel, perhaps 'American Suicide,' based on the true stories of the thousands of Iraq and Afghan vets who returned so tragically shaken by the whole truth, the whole picture.

Trump, the entertainer, understood this. He can say the shit they think and they love it. Whether Trump truly believes in his remarks is probably arguable, but the need to make those remarks, to that crowd, was obvious. He can insult Mexicans, Muslims, POWs, the disabled, women, foreign leaders, other candidates and media, even the Pope, only to the applause of that streak in American society that has always been there. This is what James Baldwin described as "The Price of the Ticket" . . . the need to demonstrate a moral awkwardness and hostile intolerance to be accepted. It applied to much of America in Baldwin's time, and while considerably less today, it is still a criterion for many republicans. For decades, we all tried to dance around the elephant in the room. Trump went over and kicked the shit out him. Apparently, money well spent.

Second, we have to show true support of the Palestinians and resolve the occupation issue. It would change so much the dynamics of the Middle East if a two-state solution is realized. Support Israel yes, of course we should, and strongly. But there is nothing that even approaches objectivity or fairness in the way major media, or congress, reacts to Israel. The sheer numbers, the facts on the ground historically and day to day do not mesh with the tone we hear in America.

The true central issue is not the resounding ceaseless refrain; Israel's right to exist or defend itself—of course it does. The central issue is, does Israel have the right to systematically expand itself? While occupying Palestinian lands with absolute control over travel, electricity, even water itself, Israel's illegal settlements leap-frog themselves. Today, close to ten percent of the entire Israeli population now live in those illegal settlements.

American media rarely address that. It is condensed into a matter of terror, strictly exhibited by Palestinians of course, and retaliation. The retaliation, no matter how brutal, systematic or terroristic itself, is invariably portrayed as justified.

When Donald Trump suggested we go after terrorists' families it was seen as outrageous by most pundits and politicians, yet Israel has been doing it for years. If a Palestinian kills an Israeli, he is not only killed or captured, but often his family, parents and siblings, lose work permits and the family's home is torn down, even law suits that could leave their young children in debt. I suppose there is an explanation somewhere there. When the Israelis rained a toxic burning chemical known as white phosphorus on the dense civilian population of Gaza in 2008-09, there was relatively little reaction from the politicians or the press. Not to mention the summer of 2014. The demographics of Gaza and the horrendous fighter jet bombing must say something. Even if Hamas had literally locked their "human shields" in place, do you kill seven hostages including three children to kill the three terrorists? "They're forcing us to kill children" was the Israeli government mantra. These kinds of action go a long way in the wrong direction. If you can be forced to kill children, with the might of a vastly superior military, you are in a fucked up place, strategically and morally. The collective punishment of a million people in Gaza, virtually half under twenty-one, is not right. None of that half in Gaza voted for Hamas, it simply wasn't possible, yet they are paying the price. I realize Hamas and the Palestinian Authority, in their battles and failures to unify, exacerbates the suffering, and as well, the Egyptian closure of the Rafah border, but there is no question the only real authority in the West Bank or Gaza is Israel.

Simply put, the coverage of that conflict, even as it goes on for decades, is woefully incomplete, generally absent of any context; the fifty-year movement to expel Palestinians from virtually any area considered "biblical" or greater Israel. If we heard what they hear in Israel itself, which maintains vigorous and realistic debate, we would at least have a bit of balance in what's reported. Most Americans are clueless about life under the occupation, for that matter, that there is an occupation. Judging the way it is presented; right to defend itself, you would think the Palestinians are occupying Israel. When one thinks of American foreign aid you might think developing countries needing roads, schools, hospitals or disaster relief. Israel is a rich, highly developed, nuclear armed country and yet receives more aid than any other, billions, virtually all to insure the overwhelming ability to protect itself from a neighboring state, as well as maintain and secure the occupation.

The unfortunate problem that has framed the issue is the notion that any critical position on Israel's positions is anti-Semitic. Anti-Semitism is real, history is replete with it, but to throw the charge at anyone, especially when it is obvious there is no rational argument, it's insulting. I do not say this easily. I have, and have had all my life, very dear Jewish friends, but this is not about religion or Jewish culture. A culture I believe values peace, scholarship, empathy, open debate and fairness. I may criticize the US, Turkish, Russian or the Chinese governments, yet I don't hate Turks or Russians or North Koreans, but when it comes to Israel, with many, it's all of a sudden personal. I hope my Jewish friends, or any Jews, not do so. This has to do with a government and its policies, and again, a deceptive narrative.

Every person understands the importance of a homeland, a foundation of themselves or their people, but do the Palestinians have no claim to some of the land they've been on for a hundred generations? The resolution of the Palestinian issue is considered by countless experts all over the world, even here, as vital in fighting radical extremists. If there is one step that would have a profound impact, it is this resolution. I know the excuses range from this being thousands of years in the making, to there is "No Partner" to make peace, but peace would take away a huge component of excuses for those who are truly anti-Semitic and anti-American. Israel exists and will exist, it is de-facto, but the land grab should not have to be. I know the word "apartheid" will trigger rage in some, and I don't know the system well enough to suggest that. Nelson Mandela knew it, "Palestine is the greatest moral issue of our age," he said.

Of course we should never abandon Israel; that is ridiculous. Just stop looking away when they do things that the entire world—except us—condemns. Jews have suffered throughout history, unimaginably in the Holocaust, and yet their ratio of contributions and accomplishment as a people are without peer. It is fact however you attribute it. Although, the Palestinians are, crazy as it sounds, human beings too. As Rabbi Hillel famously summarized the Torah, "That which is hateful to you, do not unto others, that is the Torah. The rest is commentary, go and study the commentary."

To be fair, there is another country immune to criticism that is simply beyond the pale, Saudi Arabia. The Saudis are probably as guilty as anyone for the rise of the jihadists that have led to the likes of ISIS. Saudi Wahhabism has fueled virtually every jihad extremist group over the entire world. However, the role of oil and arms is so profound, so essential to the status quo, we again look away. Look away from the beheadings they regularly, almost casually carry out, the unbelievable treatment of women, the crazy punishments for some crimes, and September 11, who knows. Even given that, they remain a close ally. But, importantly, Saudi Arabia does not call itself a democracy or tout human rights. The hypocrisy seems to be with us. In 2016, the U.S., with the Saudis, made the largest arms sale in history. The obvious trail of money to groups that are flagrantly violent towards America becomes invisible. Oh that crazy trail of money, it knows not what it does . . . you are forgiven.

———

Third, stop this crazy "War on Drugs." The irony is mind-boggling. Billions of dollars are spent developing and marketing drugs for everything from depression and impotence to coughs and calluses. We are hit over the head during the nightly news with nothing but drug ads, start to finish. And, within the newscast we often have "medical" reports. How many are done, or not done, considering interest of the main sponsors. Forget the corpulent list of side effects, the main intent is not the effect on you but on the wealth care of our health care drug industry. It used to be, the doctor would tell you what you needed and what you did not. Today, big pharma tells us to "Talk to your doctor and tell him what you want." America and New Zealand are the only countries in the world that allow this kind of direct pharmaceutical advertising. The doctors, in turn, often have been sold the same pitch by the incessant visits of drug reps. Talk about the ultimate pimps, they not only have the pushers and the junkies, they have the loan sharks . . . the complicit insurance companies. This proliferation of medication has fueled a normality of drug use. Many thousands of young boys particularly, being diagnosed with ADHD and put on a regimen of pills for years to "calm them down" and help them focus. By early adulthood it should be no surprise they easily consider medication to remedy any problem.

Things like Oxycontin, and indeed, heroin, are now reaching epidemic proportions that make the seventies look like an afternoon tea. There is another interesting aspect to this war . . . deaths. Heroin takes more lives than auto accidents, the great majority middle-class whites, and yet this huge issue was all but invisible in the political campaigns of 2016. It is seen as a public health crisis, as it should be, not so much as a crime. Perhaps it will take this kind of epidemic, affecting these kinds of people, to unlock the position that locking up drug users is the answer. Every twenty five seconds someone is arrested for possession of illegal drugs for personal use, typically marijuana. So this war on illicit drugs is very strange. What has it accomplished? Certainly one thing, the great majority of our prisons are filled with non-violent drug offenders, more of them in prison now than the entire prison population in 1970, creating the world's greatest incarceration rate. Many convicted of so-called victimless crimes. What our laws have done with the "war on drugs" has basically served to render a large portion of two generations of young black men unviable. Drug use rates of blacks and whites are the same, yet blacks are 3-7 times more likely to be arrested. African American men make up less than .08% of the world's population but make up a full 8% of the world's imprisoned. Those arrests affecting job applications, housing, voting, education assistance etc., things that make you a real threat politically, are rendered useless.

Barack Obama admits he smoked pot, even did cocaine as a young man, but he was in Hawaii with white grandparents and in college, not in the hood. Had he been stopped and frisked, the tactic so beloved by the right, and the pot been found, his ass would be where they so badly want him, out of the picture. What conceivable sense of justice provides a sentence of life without parole to a young woman for simply saying, on a tapped line, "I will see what I can do" when an informant asked if she knew where they could find some crack. I don't recall the woman's name, but I know the case is real. No drugs found, no violent behavior, just the 'three strikes law' enabled by a petulant congress. Over 3,000 people languish in life without parole because they committed a third crime, any crime . . . driving off without paying for gas or writing a bad check, might warrant the rest of life behind bars.

One of the great untold stories is the shameful business behind the prison business. The continuing shift toward private systems like The Correction Corporation of America, and the budget priorities that leave inmates with an almost pathetic healthcare system. It is hard to estimate the scale of Hepatitis-C throughout the prison populations, some say almost 40%, the incredible rate of solitary confinement, something not a part of sentencing but an operating tactic. For men and women to be held in sometimes windowless cells for 23 of 24 hours for years, even decades, is a torture we don't, and won't, see. These are not necessarily violent offenders, just prisoners the warden deems potential problems, gang members, "radicals" about race or politics. Ostensibly to protect the order or safety of the general population, it invariably leaves the inmate for the worse, whether in prison or after release.

The lobby for laws that jail offenders at such a rate is very often driven by the private sector that benefits from that high rate. Whether it's meals, or laundry, or healthcare, or construction, tough on drug crime is good on business, the prison business. We won't stop a war that demands a steady stream of product, and thereby profit, whether bombs and bullets or pills and prisoners. If we spent half the money being used to fight "the war on drugs," to rehabilitate the users and educate the youngsters, over time, a regulated decriminalized drug policy would lead to less use and less victimless crime. Many, many world leaders are calling for such a policy, but we just say no. The social imprint and the cash impact are too appealing.

And, to say the least, there is the sad brutal reality of Mexico and Central America. We are freaked out by the savage ISIL fighters of the Islamic State, and yet Americans hear only periodically of the carnage that has left over 100,000 Mexicans dead at the hands of the cartels in the last two decades. Displayed beheadings, mutilations, immolations, torture, and terror have horrified millions south of the border. The money is so vast, profit from our insatiable drug use so endless that paying off the powers when necessary is trivial.

The only solution has to come from each of us, to stop the demand. It could take a decade or more to treat the addicted and educate society so avoidance becomes, like cigarettes and alcohol, a simple understanding. Easier said than done, certainly, but after fifty years of this war it's time for a cease fire.

———————

I have talked a lot about narrative in this book, and I no doubt have my own. Is my narrative overly racial? Are my loyalties blinding? Do I sound angry? Maybe. I might be overly cynical about American hegemony in the world, yet I believe, we Americans, if we can get past our narratives, can change the world for the better. No other country has our potential, our great assembly of people. With that in mind, thinking "what if," may at times be academic, but never a waste of time.

Eleven

One day in high school, our history class spent an hour on a couple pages in our vast World History book. They described, within those two pages, an obviously obscure event in history known as the Ottoman Empire. Even at seventeen, I thought what's the deal? I saw the map of the empire covering some of Europe, the Middle East, all of northern Africa and years that spanned centuries. So much history over so much time on just two pages? I would always recall that day when I thought about how black history was neglected, as was, world history. We were taught only the story of Europeans and white Americans, which seemed the only history that mattered. It is weird how the snapshot of that page stayed in my mind for years, as if to say, remember the Ottoman Empire, one day you will really learn about it.

I have been fortunate in many ways but there is no doubt, my wife Birnur has been my Godsend. Life can sometimes give you a gift that isn't just unexpected but full and profound. I was lucky enough to not only find my loving, compassionate, kind, highly intelligent, and sexy soulmate, but she also brought a whole other world that expanded my life tremendously, Turkey. Aside from meeting many Turks here, and the exposure to their culture, I have been able to visit the country many times. I've seen other countries as result of my work: Spain, Japan, Russia, all on the level of a working visit, but in Turkey it was submergence on a home level. With family and friends who embraced me, I was not a wandering tourist; I was discovering a new home. My first trip was in the summer of 1986, we had been married about a year and made plans to visit. There had been a couple of terrorist attacks in the previous months, including a horrible shooting at the Milan, Italy airport. Some of our friends thought it would not be safe. Birnur was not phased, the notion of machine gun toting guards and dogs was a common presence at

Turkish airports, and I realized the chance of some kind of accident was far greater than terror.

We went in mid-June, and it was, to this day, the most fascinating month of my life. We arrived in Istanbul and spent a few minutes in the office of an airport manager who knew Birnur's brother. It was like a scene from Casablanca, large open windows looking out on the runways with a beautiful deep blue sky, an easy soft breeze flooding us as we sipped tea and tasted sweet pastries while our host sat back and grinned proudly, wearing his classic Turkish mustache. His office was mostly bare with just a couple chairs and a file cabinet. The ubiquitous framed picture of Ataturk, the founder of the republic, hung behind him and a small Turkish flag stood on his desk. A large old thin Turkish carpet covered the floor and above our heads a ceiling fan, that seemed just as old, hung still, unnecessary. He was very friendly and animated while he enjoyed his, as ubiquitous, cigarette. Overly accommodating, offering everything from water to use of the phone, I sensed he was impressed with himself, or maybe just happy he could be so hospitable. We chatted, or I should say they chatted, for about twenty minutes while I took in the atmosphere that was at once very familiar yet exotic, a mixture of smells and sounds and language. It seemed that just under my conscious level, I was constantly recalibrating my reference of normal. There was something about it that made me feel childlike, wishing I could just run with my arms and eyes wide open with a giddiness of an eight-year-old.

Soon, we were walking on the tarmac to the plane for the early evening flight to the Aegean pearl, Izmir. Birnur was beside herself with happiness, anxious to be home again. When we neared Izmir she became teary-eyed as we flew over the brown and green land of ancient mythology: Troy, Ephesus, and the biblical city of Smyrna now Izmir, her birthplace. Her mother was there to greet us and we took a cab to her home passing carts pushed by men and pulled by donkeys, filled with things like kitchenware or melons or bread. My first impression was surprise; I had forgotten that Turkey, in many respects, was still a Third World country. However, I soon found as we got closer into town the very modern world of any city in the US. I encountered such a range in everything. You might see a man riding in a donkey pulled cart next to a man driving a new Mercedes, or a woman covered with a scarf and long coat next to young women in mini-skirts. Like anybody in a far away land, I was stimulated with each breath. The sounds and smells and sites were all so fascinating.

If the time at the airport was like a movie, the next morning was indeed dreamlike. I woke up about 5 am and heard a moaning yet song-like voice from outside. It was the call of the Imam, or priest. The chants wafted from each direction, voices from mosque minarets close and far dotting the neighborhoods, nudging the faithful to the first prayer of the day. I walked to the window and saw the light of the sun begin to peek over the low mountains. The colors were unbelievable pastels of purple and orange with white to yellow highlights from a few feathery clouds. Birds chirped to each other in the trees, and the breeze, the ever-present breeze from the bay, seem to bring the sounds and colors to me so softly it was like the hand of God Himself. It was utterly unforgettable. We all have references of some sort to define something as sublime, whether from movies or books or even dreams, it strikes a chord in your soul you just feel. I felt something infinite about that moment. It was the first of many remarkable things I would experience. For about four or five years, I remembered each full day of that month-long trip, every lunch, every shop, every beach, every relative I met. It was the first of a dozen trips I deeply treasure.

Turkish people are extremely warm and hospitable, especially in the small towns and villages you travel through on your way to popular tourist or resort destinations. Most years we visited Bodrum, an ancient town once known as Halicarnassus, on the southwest Aegean coast. Bodrum is the town Birnur and her family would visit when she was a child, holding a very special place in her heart, and today, ours. An incredible spot of history and beauty, it has a large castle built by the Knights of Saint John in the early sixteenth century. The setting is like something from the TV series "Game of Thrones," rolling hills with an ancient amphitheater looking out over the bay, with the castle sitting on a peninsula jutting out into the center, holding watch over the Aegean. An icon of Turkish recreation and "hedonistic" travelers, it was once just a small fishing village, like many on the vast Aegean and Mediterranean coast. That little village has evolved into one of the hottest vacation spots for Europeans. In 1986, it was beginning to attract the likes of Mick Jagger, Madonna, and many of Europe's who's who, becoming a best kept secret for the 'jet set'. Nevertheless, it remains oblivious to some of the most sophisticated American travelers.

Bodrum, in the eighties and nineties was, and I suppose still to an extent, a real blend of playground and fascinating exploration. The harbor lined with boats twenty to a hundred feet long, was divided at points to separate the private, and often luxurious, yachts from the workboat stables that toured for tourist. Most in modest condition, they were put to task probably nine of ten days for the hundreds of tourist, Germans and Brits mostly. By early evening, the small streets would fill with the freshly bathed and burned skin of Europeans on the hunt for fun. Hunting for dinner, hunting for souvenirs, hunting for that unlikely but possible treasure from a kind old vendor. The main stretch, or street, paved in stones hundreds of years old or only a few weeks, ran from the foot of the ancient castle along the shore as it curved around the bay. Along the way countless little shops and displays of Turkish charms and jewelry, silver and leather goods, clothing, and of course food. But the side and back streets of this two thousand year port was where you'd more likely find the treasures, not just in silver or antiques, but the people, the older locals who had seen this little village turn into a spectacle in their lifetime.

Virtually all the shoreline on the other side of those shops held restaurants, one after another. Tables and chairs and the constant movement of men in white shirts and black pants serving patrons, sometimes literally while in the softly lapping water at their feet. At the end of the perhaps half mile stretch, fancy neon-loaded indoor and outdoor discos. Filled late into the night with young, energetic and carefree vacationers, they kicked off the transformation of Bodrum into a commercial attraction. From Bodrum, or anywhere on the coast, you could enjoy the immaculate weather and seas for only a few dollars at that time. The Greek isles are well touted and very popular, yet Americans don't realize the majority of those mythic and beautiful playgrounds of the rich are closer to the Turkish mainland than Greece. Today, as Turkey has become more known, and with a stronger economy, the cost is comparable. Still, the experience is incomparable, with a landscape far less spoiled by trampling tourist, clear footsteps remain of three great empires, and sacred biblical points. There we saw the great landmarks and landscapes of ancient mythology, yet, it was home for Birnur.

The trip to Bodrum could take close to five hours, given the roads in 1986, slowly winding around mountains and passing through small towns that dotted the ancient landscape. Roman aqueducts and Greek ruins, castles and walls from the ancient Hittites, all creating a dreamscape for a history buff. I wished I could stop the bus and walk up into the hillside, through the olive trees and rock, to see and touch the timeless structures. On trips in later years, with a rental car, I would. That part of the Turkish coast on the Aegean is so beautiful. The blend of weather, history, sea, and scenery is unique. The coast is full of spots to swim in clear blue seas and enjoy the colorful fish and amazing ruins from Greek and Roman periods that you can touch underwater. In the evenings, we would walk through small towns and shop, as well as eat and drink a very long dinner, watching what seemed to be a timeless dusk from evening to night.

Our trips had endless meals with family and friends. Lunch was planned, literally, while we finished breakfast. Cousins and aunts, friends, and friends of cousins and aunts, would prepare feast of classic Turkish dishes that could last hours, with endless servings of tea. Some hours, for me, were spent in somewhat solitude, watching faces express the sentiment of words I couldn't understand, but I was never bored or neglected. There was also fascination at the homes, with various Turkish motifs of antiquity as well as modern marble, crystal and leather. The sheer age of things could be amazing to an American; we think something is old if it is over a hundred years. In Turkey, buildings, roads and even furniture might be hundreds of years and still used every day. I've always enjoyed history, and being immersed in a place so immersed in history was really a treat. It was also introspective, as a Black American, to think of the disconnect from my history, from whichever root, and yet, here feel a kinship with the ages.

Istanbul, at its most glorious point, was the most envied city in the world. By the 18th century it was the place to pursue any desire, whether sensual or intellectual. The seat of a vast empire that had once threatened much of Europe, it was lavished in splendor and excess to demonstrate Ottoman dominance. Ruled by a series of all powerful sultans, the Turks were the object of total disdain or total fascination by Europeans. Somewhat fascinating to me, a black African would be in the circle of the three or four most powerful under the sultan. The chief black eunuch controlled the harem, the finances of the imperial mosques, and himself had almost unequalled access to the sultan. In many of the great paintings depicting the various sultans and his court, there is a unique black face among the Turks.

———

That grand empire ended after four hundred years with the First World War and the creation of Turkey in 1923. Its borders now confined to the land mass known, geographically, as Asia Minor or Anatolia. Mustafa Kemal, or Ataturk, is considered one of the great figures of the twentieth century for not only saving the homeland of the Ottomans but simultaneously breaking from it as well. He called for a western oriented modernization, changing the alphabet, the fashions, the education of women, and the removal of religion from government. The, what some call, "turn away" from its past has always been an issue in Turkey, mostly framed around religious perspectives and cultural traditions, always debating what it means to be Turkish. For decades, the army had always acted, sometimes with murderous coups, as the enforcement of a secular government.

Today, it has been purged of any who have been, or might be, critical of the current political power. The recent attempted coup in the summer of 2016 displayed the broken state of loyalty in the army, and, increasingly in society. That, and other signals of a more religious orientation by the leaders, has many worried it might "turn away" from its secular history. The party of Tayyip Erdogan, the prime minister, and now president, has hinted it will realize an Islamic Republic of Turkey one day. What has not been a hint is his virtual role of dictator, jailing journalists for any criticism, fighting wars within and outside of Turkey, overseeing crony corruption that's shocking by any measure.

Now, after the coup attempt, whole segments of civil society are being labeled traitors, dismissed from their jobs or even arrested. I fear what lies ahead for my family and friends if that mentality continues. In their resentment of the secular decades that they believe restricted "true" Turkish culture, a strong nationalist character is growing, though too vengeful, too fast. That said, Turkey saw dynamic economic growth in the first decade of the twenty-first century. Unfortunately, it appears much of it involved government corruption and bribery, but like everywhere, loyalties to a narrative about oneself, however tainted, run deep. Birnur's brother, Onur and his wife, Mine, are seeing the country change and worry for the future of their lovely young daughter, Saba. It is not out of the question that they might move. We are all hopeful Turkey will get past this crisis, peacefully. A blend of east and west, modern and traditional, the Turkish identity is complex, and contentious, but all are proud to be Turks.

It is less apparent today, but the economic disparity always bothered me when I visited the first few times. In the cities especially, the image of people, often children, scrambling to sell almost anything from water to whistles or simply begging under ragged and filthy clothing was painful. The bus stations were always a place they were seen, appealing to tourist or Turks. Women holding sleeping, or seemingly weak, babies would follow and beg for just a coin. I was told that it was often a racket, that they would make decent money using kids and babies for sympathy. However, many times the misfortune was glaring, yet seen by everyday Turks as just everyday life in their country, unfortunately.

I remember on my first visit, we took a bus from Izmir to Bodrum and the station was bustling with all kinds of movement. Men in their sixties selling lotto tickets, young sandal clad tourist with backpacks, families slowly moving about with large sacks tied with string, the very young and the very old trying to sell something to those who looked foreign. Appealing to a Turk would typically be met with a "tskk" sound and a stiff upward jerk of the head, which means no or disagreement. Those looking affluent or foreign might try to politely avoid or motion "no" but the sell was relentless, followed in every turn to get, if only, a coin. On the bus, oddly, something was free or at least provided with the ticket. A young man would walk down the aisle holding a bottle of a lemon scented alcohol based freshener. People would hold out their hands and receive a splash that they would wipe about their hands and perhaps pat their face. Soon the travelers might feel a bit renewed.

This type of freshener, or cleanser of sort, can be seen all over Turkey, from restaurant bathrooms to courthouses, but is a certainty on bus trips. I always sat next to the window to see the things the Turks would ignore as they settled into sleep or a newspaper. The lemon scent would softly come and go as the driver maneuvered beside and around other buses, cars, newspaper stands and people, by inches.

We pulled from the station and the grumpy old engine of the aged bus moaned with resignation over yet another trip. I looked through the soft dust and noticed a handful of people on the roadside just outside the gates of the terminal. Those, who for whatever reason were not allowed in the station, were standing and staring toward the bus with envy. As the bus rocked and swung slowly to the left my eyes saw something I will never forget. A young man barely twenty, with no legs and from my view no hips, was pulling himself along on a flat piece of stiff cardboard. His tattered and filthy clothes seemed almost unnecessary given the naked cruelty. His hands and knuckles wrapped in cloth for protection, he would pivot on them to drag his torso across the gravel and dirt. He swung one arm up, palm open, begging like others I had seen but with almost certain futility. The others moved around him unfazed, as if he was a light pole. The view only lasted a few seconds but the impact has never left me, nor the context of any burdens of mine. Our eyes met for a moment and I saw his agony, not the acting of a nine year old that has learned to pull at heart strings, but pitiful truth. Years later I learned there is a rare condition in which the spine does not fully develop before birth, causing the loss of legs and perhaps hips, one man with such a condition even achieved a bit of celebrity on a tabloid TV show.

But, for this kid, there was no help. I felt an absolute shame, a true sense of failure, not so much of myself but for man as a whole. I know now, and I knew then, that scenes like that exist all over the world, that life is not fair. The difference was being a part of the scene, seeing the eyes of that whole world in his face. It magnified an impossible empathy and a reasonable question . . . we can't do better than this, yet? It was not a reflection on Turks, just life itself. My mother would say, "There, but for the grace of God, go I." A grace seemingly without rhyme or reason, unless, perhaps, to test *our* grace.

Birnur and I would take several trips to Turkey before we had kids. Each time was a wonderful time of party and sea and sun. We were usually able to take an entire month off, which passed all too quickly. Izmir was always visited, it is Birnur's home and where her mother still lives. It is such a beautiful place. I can only imagine how Birnur feels today. It must be truly heartbreaking for her think about how her life would be if we could have lived there all these years. Birnur left at the young age of twenty-three and never moved back. And, certainly, it must have been, and is, a terrific heartbreak for her mother, Nur. Only five years earlier, Nur lost Birnur's father, Orhan, of a heart attack at age forty eight, leaving her with two teenage children. Birnur loves Turkey, and never in her dreams did she believe she would spend her life in Atlanta, but she did, because of me. If I could wish for one thing besides the happiness of my children, and a recovery from this difficult health battle, it would be to spend a long retirement in Izmir, and those small simple places on the Aegean, my wife's home.

Over twenty years or so, we would visit often. It was certainly the happiest time for us. Melody and Orman would enjoy the beaches and pools of course, but I also believe it was exciting for them to travel on the planes and buses and see and hear a different kind of world. Nineteen ninety nine was a very memorable trip, Istanbul was changing, a beautiful new airport, new roads, skyscrapers, and Birnur's brother, Onur, had a new home complete with a pool. It was, although, still Turkey. His home was on a street with other nice homes, but only a stone's throw from the poor, living in very old and often dilapidated houses. Onur was very successful with his business and enjoyed a lifestyle reserved for the top two percent of Turks. They had a live-in nanny for their son, Genco, a gardener, a housekeeper, a chauffeur, and the finest food, clothes and cars. The help was inexpensive, with any job for the uneducated hard to get, you could hire three people for less than one would cost in the states.

There were some who walked the streets all day selling fruits or simply water to earn a few liras. I remember the repetitive calls of one man in particular selling 'simit', the famous round ring-like sesame topped bread. Each morning and thru the day, he walked the streets. In his late forties, tall and muscular with movie star looks, he pushed his small cart up and down the hilly neighborhoods, calling out "simmeeeyet" every five or ten seconds. He was such a sad character, so handsome and seemingly intelligent, with a very melancholy and resigned look, walking and working so hard for so little. It was again so eye opening, the comparison of struggle and poverty that redefined what I knew till then. Not that a condition like that is not in the US, but it was such a normal sight right next to the Mercedes floating by. Birnur's family was among the privileged and educated, with ties from Ottoman ruling class; her great-great grandfather had been the governor of what is now Syria. Her father, Orhan Koca, worked in the tobacco business, and with their mom, Nur, provided an education that is everything in Turkey, nourishing a high intellect in both children. Still, historically, it is not the best social equation to have such broad gaps, things happen. It was something that always struck me as so unbalanced and precarious. How ever honestly earned or justly deserved, to live and feast upon the sweetest cake while so many struggled for simple bread, was uncomfortable for me.

———————

That 'blend' in Turkey is everywhere, with everything. Often described, 'east meeting west,' it is very diverse. A Muslim country, it is secular, with rare though nonetheless topless beaches and the most western motifs. Yet, it's not at all disconnected from its iconic Ottoman history. Depending on where you are, the Muslim culture can be subtle or very demanding. At the resorts and tourist attractions, you have very western styles and systems, but out in the large spans of countryside you may see truckloads of women coming and going from the fields. Women, for the most part, harvest those fields, covered almost entirely with colorful loose pants, called shalvar, blouses and scarves. Meanwhile, you might see the men in small villages sitting at coffee shops sipping tea and smoking. From the outside, it may seem another example of the role women play in the Muslim world, but I can't say it is solely a consequence of religion. Women, in Turkey, were given the right to vote as early as America's women, and there has even been a woman Prime Minister. Although Birnur is an atheist, I have become fairly familiar with some of the customs and traditions, and like most religion, to me; it has some 'splainin' to do. Funerals are always unique to various religions, and that summer of nineteen ninety-nine, I had the sad reason to attend one in Turkey.

We were in Bodrum with the kids having a great time, with food, fun and sun. Melody was starting to grow into an even more beautiful young girl, and Orman, about three at the time, kept us laughing. One evening we got a call, it was Debbie, Birnur's closest friend back home. She and her husband, Kerim Zamangil, a Turk, had two children as well. We were all best friends and seemed to do everything together, seeing each other as real family. Debbie told us some bad news, Kerim's mother, Rezzan, had died. Kerim immediately flew to Turkey for the funeral which, I believe according to Islam, should be done within three days. We were heading back to Istanbul the next day and Birnur thought I should fly to Ankara to be with Kerim and his family. I flew out early the morning after we returned and made it to their family home in Ankara before noon. Kerim had arrived earlier and was out trying to arrange a coffin for his mother's burial. Traditionally, the body is transported in the coffin, actually just a simple wooden box, but interred only covered in cloth. However, Kerim knew his mother wanted to be in a coffin next to his father, also in that manner. Before that, he would make sure she was washed, or cleansed, another tradition or rite which was uncomfortable for Kerim, not simply because he was not a practicing Muslim. It was hardly the kind of task we would see here by family on the day of burial. I was surprised at how casually everyone was dressed, as I was in my jacket and tie. It was going to be a very hot day and so I left the jacket before we headed to the mosque.

The mosque, in the heart of Ankara, was tremendous, it seemed to cover several square blocks. It was almost glowing from all the white marble reflecting the hot July sun. Before too long, Kerim arrived in a little pickup-type truck. Green, with a small domed cover over the bed, it was obviously a hearse of sort. Kerim was dressed sporty with jacket and sun glasses. We greeted each other like any other time, only different. About seven or eight men removed the simple wooden box and carried Rezzan to an area on the side of the mosque, not inside. It was put beside another already there. Apparently, there would be more than one service. There were two groups of people, all men, waiting for the Imam to finish noon prayers before coming out to perform services for us. The heat was worsening and everyone was huddled in a narrow shade under a small awning. When prayers were over inside, and the Imam came to us, all the men lined up in rows about five deep. I, not having a clue what would happen, did what others did. The Imam began prayers in Arabic as the men put their hands to their ears, and then cup them in front of their faces as they repeated, or perhaps responded to the Imam. Looking to one side then the other, there was a physical ritual as they spoke. It was done several times and I did my best to mimic the whole thing. My prayer was that I didn't appear as stupid as I felt, although I wanted to participate in the tribute and offer my own respect and wishes for Rezzan. The same ceremony was held for each family, and then the men took the coffins back to the truck.

A half hour away was the cemetery, an ancient area of large and small headstones and mausoleums dating back hundreds of years. At the grave site, I saw Kerim talking to the Imam, who is raising his eyebrows, rolling his eyes and sighing. It seems the Imam was not happy to make Kerim happy, either about what to say or do. After plenty of mild gesticulating, he ultimately gave in. That seemed to be an issue this whole morning, weighing the wishes of the personal against the religious or cultural guides. There again I saw what defines Turkey, this effort to balance a society of shifting parts. At this point, everyone has arrived and Kerim climbs up and straddles the grave or tomb actually. Kerim's dad was interred on one side and it was time to rest his mother beside him. It is a concrete box, partly below ground, partly above, with a small opening on top. Down inside, a worker is already crouched to receive and place the body. But Kerim is first trying to put the empty coffin in place. The space is very tight and several minutes go by and they cannot seem to maneuver it in, going inch by inch. The heat is brutal and Kerim, still wearing his jacket and sun glasses, is sweating hard. He shoves repeatedly while the worker down inside, sweating even worse, groans while he pulls and wiggles. It seemed it was not going to happen and relatives cried and looked away from the dusty scene. Kerim was undaunted, determined his mother would rest in her coffin. He continued and at one point, while leaning over, a shower of half million and million lira notes fell from his jacket. Everyone seemed frozen in the heat, enduring the frustrating sight of Kerim grabbing up fistfuls of dirt and bills with one hand, pushing it all back into pockets, as the sweat burned his eyes. All the while, the Imam is sitting on the ground a few feet away, singing prayers. It was a very powerful moment, as moving as almost anything I had seen in the TV business. And, the power of Rezzan's son prevailed as the plain wooden box found its angle and was placed inside.

Now, more than enough men, including me, stepped up to help gently place her into the coffin. Kerim and his sisters softly tossed dirt and flowers over her before the concrete lid was slid into place. Kerim sat down under a tree, covered in dust and sweat, breathing heavily and pushing his hands over his head, totally beat. His dark sunglasses hid the whole story. After a few minutes, it was back to normal; hands out . . . grave workers, drivers, the Imam, the little boys that rinsed the headstone, all looked for their lira, some just one million (about two dollars at the time), others much more. Most earned it, but some seemed to come from nowhere, perhaps a form of panhandling, showing up at funerals pretending to do something. A group of us (men) went to a small open-air cafe in a park nearby. Nestled in a grove of poplar trees, we sat mostly quiet enjoying a soft breeze. Then, it was time for a cold beer. This was, after all, Turkey. I flew back to Istanbul that same night.

Very sadly, it was only a short year before the threat of death would strike Kerim again; Debbie was diagnosed with ovarian cancer. It was unbelievable, it could not be happening; Debbie was only forty-two. They had two young kids, who were and are, almost as much ours as Debbie and Kerim's: Ayla, then twelve, and little Kerim, ten. It was a large tumor that required many doses of radiation. Debbie was always a very cheerful, carefree soul, and while she and Kerim must have endured impossible heartbreak, she carried on with an optimistic and casual demeanor. After a short remission, she grew worse and by the summer of 2001 her bad days were most days. By December, she would get regular visits from family and friends old and new. I remember one day we were over, as others were, and Debbie looked at me and said, "Wow, everybody is coming to see me, it must be bad, huh?" and she smiled. The courage was more than I had ever seen, to maintain calm in the face of losing her life, leaving two young children and a husband, was like God's grace exuding from her.

On Saturday the 22nd, her parents and relatives and close friends said goodbye. She was unconscious and breathing very shallow, but we hoped she felt our love. The house was filled with soft whimpers and attempts at philosophy, and condolence. About 2:30 that afternoon the hospice attendant let everyone know Debbie had passed. Her now 11 yr old son, little Kerim, who was tremendously attached to her, walked swiftly to his room. I followed him, not knowing what to say or do, but thinking I should. He was standing with his back against the window in his room. Still and looking down, he had a look of anger, disbelief, hurt. We all share that look a few times in life; that horrible desire to not believe, not know. His eyes blinked while he looked at the floor, hands close to his sides like he was trying to fit in a narrow space. I tried to console him, let him know he would be OK, that Debbie was OK. He showed no reaction, just a subtle motion of withdrawal, never saying a word. I didn't know what to do. I left him alone and felt I had failed. How can one not fail with something like that. Debbie was a mother, a sister, a wife and daughter, her loss left deep wounds. Birnur as well was so very heartbroken, she was not herself for many weeks.

For the Zamangils, difficult years followed and more followed those. Little Kerim, his dad and sister, Ayla, each remain very dear in our lives. Years later, I'm sure they endure their own imprint from that tragedy, an imprint that probably serves or curses them, randomly. Around 2007, Kerim found a new partner, now wife, Daneez, from Pakistan. Our families continue to be, practically one.

Twelve

I am not able to convey my story of marriage, kids and family in a competent manner. It is so life changing, not in a way of some extraordinary experiences that might occur in your life; those things may have impact but rarely in an absolute sense. Children do. When you have a child, your reference of life changes. We all know love for our spouses, parents, dear friends, and for life itself, but the love one feels for their child is a pure love, an absolute and infinite love. In fact, the word love may be insufficient. A force or will in us that would move you to give your life without the hesitation of single heartbeat somehow seems beyond love. Birnur and I were married almost five years before Melody was born. They were really fun years, trips to Turkey, cruises, jaunts to New York or New Orleans. But by our fifteenth year it was hard to remember life before kids. Priorities, focus, purpose, all had Melody and Orman at the center. Their activities: ballet, piano, basketball, swimming and the difficult financial sacrifice of a private school made life before children seem distant. The fascinating and rewarding pleasure of seeing them grow and respond to life is part of the gift of parenthood.

Melody was simply an angel, in every way. Orman was the little devil, every bit as lovable but always determined about what he wanted. I used to say that he was the littlest man I knew. He never had any doubt about his position on things. With almost six years between them, there was a long time with Melody as our center. When she was just two months old, it was difficult to leave her with a sitter but we were very lucky. Through a friend at work we met Carol Zuidema. Carol was about fifty and lived not too far from our work. She and her husband Jim became, and remain, virtual grandparents to Melody and Orman. They bonded so well with them. Melody and Orman spent many long days there over the course of those years, we were very fortunate. Today, they remain Grammy and PopPop.

Melody began kindergarten at a place called Canterbury. It was started by a woman back in the fifties and was basically a few houses that had been joined together with a common playground. It was a bit rustic; in fact some found it a bit hazardous, as the aging houses and grounds were not exactly state of the art. However, the teachers and Mrs. Bush, the founder, were warm and more like a family than a school. Many days I would be the last to pick up Melody, often a half to an hour late, but Mrs. Bush was there, in their cozy little library with her. It had to be tough sometimes for Melody to be the last, usually, to be picked up but she never complained, my angel. We would talk all the way home, sometimes listening to a radio talk show called 'My Word,' a British word-game show we enjoyed. She was always saying those things that tickle a parent. Once, I told her that I was 38 years old, "Pretty old" I said. She replied, "Thirty-eight's not old daddy, there are lots of people older than 38 . . . You just look old". I laugh to this day about the benign honesty she would deliver. Another time on the way home she asked me incredulously, "daddy, did you know Michael Jackson is black?" Ironically, I'm not sure if at that point she was aware that we were black.

Orman was no different, but his humor was usually more intentional, his wit was remarkable for a kid. Once at dinner when he was about five he accidentally flipped his entire plate over and food flew everywhere. He casually turned his head with a smile and one eye cocked and said "I meant to do that".

They were typical in many ways. Melody loved dolls and playing princess, wanting everything in pink and loving ballerinas. She had, and has, a very strong artistic ability, whether drawing and painting or decorating, although she never kept her room the most graceful. She made us so proud of her voice and talent. In the eighth grade, she amazed crowds at school in her lead role in 'Pirates of Penzance,' as well as other performances. She has always loved books, then and now. And, she loves children, working on becoming a teacher. Although, she also loves the idea of interior decorating. We'll have to see where her heart leads.

Orman loved toy cars, toy lions, and any kind of sport. He was a real fan of Zorro, and movies that had sword fighting, loving the physical acrobatics of the hero. Athletic ability comes natural to him and he excels in virtually any sport he gets involved in. He has always had an uncanny recall; scenes from movies, sports stats or something I might have said months before. Once when he was around sixteen, I was telling him about Reggie Jackson, a famous ballplayer from my teens, he instantly broke in; "Reggie Jackson, Mr. October, 563 home runs, twice World Series MVP, where he smacked four consecutive home runs, three on three pitches . . ." I was stunned, "Man, you are something" I said, just amazed. He sat there a moment and grinned, nodding with a "yeah, I know" sigh. Then he laughed and said "Actually dad, it was a scene from a movie, 'Benchwarmers.' I laughed as I pretended to strangle him, still amazed. He's now working on his degree in the physical sciences, but I think his calling is talking.

We did a lot together on the weekends, many times going to Stone Mountain Park where we would walk our dogs, Joey and Charlie. We would fish at a trout farm, ride our bikes, and visit an animal farm called The Yellow River Game Ranch where we could see many tamed creatures like deer and donkeys as well as buffalo behind fences. The summers always included trips to Florida at a place in Destin called The Pelican Beach Resort. Turkey, of course, was a trip every other year. Birnur's mother would visit on the off year. I don't know what they think of those days in Turkey, they meant different things to each of us. I was fascinated with everything about it, Birnur was "going home" and sometimes redefining it. To Melody and Orman it was probably an exciting plane ride, then a weird language, and lots of eating and walking, and the sea and boats. It would be interesting to know what snapshots in their memories they will have in their forties. Fortunately, for them and us, I shot hours and hours of video from those trips and outings. The thought of them sharing those scenes with their grandchildren is remarkable.

Something they will also have in memory and video is "The Children's Holiday." When Birnur was a child, she enjoyed an annual celebration in Turkey known as Children's Day. It was begun decades earlier by Mustafa Kemal Ataturk, Turkey's founder. It was to recognize and celebrate children and their importance. There would be parades and music, food and costumes. We have several pictures of Birnur and her brother on that holiday when they were kids. When Melody was about three, Birnur wanted her to have a celebration. So in the kitchen of Carol's home we had a "Children's Day" with about a dozen kids, cake and ice cream. The next year Birnur got other Turks involved and we were granted cafeteria space at a church near Carol's. Birnur called local schools that had other ethnic student groups and asked if they would join and share their cultural songs or dances, etc. It was a big success. By the sixth or seventh year, we had hundreds of participants and it was even recognized by UNICEF. And, we had a mayor that proclaimed "April 23, Turkish Children's Day in Atlanta." A core group of about 10-15 Turks and Americans decorated and built an experience for all kids that came. Held on the weekend around the 23rd of April, we had displays of Turkish carpets and copper, posters and T-shirts, flags and flowers. Before the performances, children were urged to visit many booths that displayed things of different countries, with maps, pictures and fun facts. The kids would receive a "passport" to have stamped as they visited and learned about the countries in each booth.

We eventually called it "International Children's Day." It was still a mostly Turkish celebration, but lots of music and dance and performance from Panamanian, Chinese, Nigerian, German and others as well as plenty of Turkish kids and sometimes adults. Melody and Orman would always have roles introducing acts or awarding door prizes, after all, mom was the founder, even got on TV most years. But, after 12 yrs their interest waned and Birnur found it hard to keep it going as the children, of those who were putting in the hard work each year, grew up. Around 2009, with my condition getting difficult, we left it to others in the Turkish community. Today, it continues but not as grand, and virtually all Turkish. I am so proud of Birnur for that amazing event, and her impact on the way the children saw each other, something hundreds of them will remember a long time, maybe a lifetime.

Turkey was, and is, by far the most fascinating place I've been. The incredible history alone can keep a history buff amazed for months. The culture of kindness and hospitality seems almost overdone, until you realize how central it is to family life there. And, the food and climate explain why it has been treasured by those who have lived there. I'm sure there are places that are just as special, but it is hard to say. After all, as I mentioned, I have only spent time in three other countries: Spain, Russia, and Japan.

I was in Barcelona for three weeks for the 1992 Summer Olympics. It was fabulous. We sent three crews to the games, one to cover the Atlanta Olympic Planning Committee that would host the games four years later, another to cover events and athletes, and me with a reporter to cover Barcelona, sweet. It was the best single time I ever had working. It was hot, and we did a lot of walking, but Barcelona was beautiful. We toured the tourist spots like the Sagrada Familia, the fascinating, and at the time still unfinished, landmark of the Barcelona skyline. And Tibidabo park, an amusement park built on top of Tibidabo Mountain overlooking the city. It's an amazing site at night. The famous Ramblas, the large main avenue that is the centerpiece for strolling, shopping and dining, was our usual evening hangout. We met locals and saw what the homes are like with typical foods and drink. And, we also followed the "beautiful people", the celebrities and politicians and athletes that ran about town enjoying the multi-million dollar yachts and the outrageously expensive night life. I also worked with our famous NBC colleagues like, as I mentioned, O.J. Simpson. I got to know Katie Couric fairly well. Young, and early in her career, she really enjoyed her job as anchor and was an easy performer for the camera. I was "Hoov" to her, my name tag I.D said Hoover, she thought it was a neat name but too formal, she liked nicknames.

Japan was also exciting and fascinating. I went in 1986 to cover three basketball games. The Georgia Tech team was part of a tournament sponsored by Suntori, a Japanese liquor company. Aside from shooting the three games and practice, we followed the team around sightseeing. Japan was going through its economic heyday and we stayed at a very swank hotel in Ginza, probably the most iconic spot in Tokyo. Japan had some very interesting cultural situations. A very modern and cosmopolitan place, yet not disconnected from tradition. Everything appeared so clean and orderly, even work crews wore white gloves and tried to be as neat as possible. Many people could be seen walking around with masks for covering their mouths, not to spread germs. The older women were often seen in older traditional Kimono dresses, while younger women proudly carried themselves in skirts or a western professional look. Electronics were exploding in Tokyo, with shops everywhere selling all the latest gadgets, games and cameras. The prices displayed more predominately than the product, jumping at you with color and art. The "pop" art was very aggressive everywhere, as if to say "look, it's 1986, Japan is back!"

There seemed to be a juggling of moral norms. In the hotel I stayed there were nude magazines available, but the photographs had been retouched. The private areas of women had been scratched away, not on the page literally, but in some post production. At the same time, prostitutes were allowed to solicit at the hotel. It was not official of course, and not more than a few, but staff looked away. I suppose it was considered an accommodation. Several times I was followed into the elevator by mature women, perhaps in their early forties appearing to be on business, who would wait for the door to close and ask, in their very Japanese manner of a polite yet earnest host, "you need ah company to-night?". It was unlike any fancy hotel I have ever stayed. I guess it was a high-end hotel like others around the world, a man's world. Japan's world was certainly something center stage at the time. But with all the sophistication, it was still the Japan in the pictures. The beautiful wooden architecture and gardens, large carved artworks and the delicate beauty of silk. There was quite a basketball tournament, too.

I know a little of Russian history and the talent of Russian people, especially their music, but I was never curious enough to imagine going there one day. The fall of the Soviet Union was probably inevitable, given human nature, but still sad for those around the world who hold some version of socialism as a means of helping those like the legless man I saw at that bus station in Izmir. Communism, I believe, was an attempt to help man, despite himself and despite the nature of man. While it may be in man's nature to be empathetic and sympathetic, it is also in his nature to be greedy and egotistical, and more to the point with Russia, in his nature to grow and develop himself and realize the rewards of that growth. That nature, burdens a communist society. Unfortunately, it seems that human nature may also destroy Capitalism. The greed and ego that seems central to the so-called free market system leads to the other end of failure: Extreme and all powerful wealth. Where, with only rare exception, the growth and development of money or capital has usurped, overruled, disregarded and all but forgot anything that might oblige our fellow man. Churchill again might say "never have so few held so much at the expense of so many."

Hopefully, we won't see what I saw in Moscow in 1991. I was there with a group known as 'The Friendship Force.' Each year this organization would send a group of families or friends to a foreign country to establish friendships. We went along with a group from the Atlanta chapter. I was with a reporter and friend, Donna Lowry. We were staying with a host family, who thought we were married, so they had to make some quick switches to the sleeping arrangements, but it worked out and it was a fascinating experience. Our hosts, Vladimir and Ludmila Kuznetsov were well-educated. She was in law and Vladimir an engineer. Vladimir was also in the Army as well, where he served as an engineer but also in the regular units. As part of our assignment, we profiled the family and their daily life in a progressively failing Soviet state. Both about forty, with two daughters and a young son, they were very hopeful about the new direction Russia was taking. Their flat was relatively small but sufficient for them, even able to accommodate us, and was probably like millions of others in the country. It was close to Christmas when we were there, and we went along with them to work and shopping. Moscow in December is cold and snowy, making hauling a TV news camera around effortless . . . easy work. I tagged along with Vladimir on his way to work one morning and was struck by the blank faces on the streets. People standing at bus stations, walking by or in the small old Ladas they drove, still and quiet, almost oblivious to the cameraman with the soldier, or anything else for that matter. They were unfazed, one way or the other, at anything. Covered in long coats and the ubiquitous ushanka fur hats, they seemed on a kind of auto-pilot, resigned to the terribly difficult years leading to this point. Everywhere the entire country seemed to be on low power, from the streetlights to the car lights, to the light in the eyes of the people, it was dreary. The short winter days with snow everywhere and the exhaust of vehicles made the atmosphere heavy and seem motionless. The buildings and almost all structures looked fifty years old at least, and without maintenance for the last twenty.

This was the beginning of the end. The Soviet Union was collapsing. Wherever we went, whether a small butcher shop or what was the largest department store in Russia, the scene was predictable . . . empty shelves, literally empty. I went into a small shop with Vladimir one morning to look for meat, and there were only two or three pieces on shelves that could hold a hundred or more. Vladimir, like me, knowing only a few words of each other's language, simply broke a weak smile and raised his eyebrows. It may have been the time of day or day of the week, but his look told me otherwise. In a few days, the day after Christmas, the Soviet Union was no more. Few were given advance notice when the Soviet flag, with its sickle and hammer, would come down from the top of the Kremlin shortly after midnight. We had been in Red Square that day after Christmas 1991 shooting the crowds of locals, and tourist, keeping a third eye on the flag, but we were not there for that story. Nonetheless, I feel I witnessed a very historic moment of the twentieth century. I left Russia with admiration for the level of literacy and education most people seemed to have, whether misguided by propaganda or not, they aren't stupid. Everyone was glad to see a change, to see opportunity given to that potential.

Literacy and education are such an important part of society, an informed society is a healthy society. The wise man was asked, "What is the meaning of wisdom?" he said "Good judgement," "Then what is the secret of good judgement?," he said "Experience," "And what is the secret of experience?" The wise man said "Bad judgement." While nothing is more important than a good education, we live and learn most beyond our schools, often through experience. In 1977, when I met Maynard Jackson, I saw what education, intellect and "good judgement" could mean for black people, for any people. Maynard was exceptional, graduating from Morehouse at age 18, passing the bar at 21; he seemed wise beyond his young thirty-five years when he was elected mayor of Atlanta in 1973. First black mayor was a job some may have thought daunting. Atlanta, after all, was the jewel of the south. This was where Gone With The Wind premiered in 1939, twenty miles from Stone Mountain, the supposed birthplace of the Klan. Atlanta, the birthplace of

Martin Luther King Jr., called itself "The city too busy to hate," yet threats to this courageous bright young mayor were constant. The power structure of this "busy" city found itself with a black city government that would not continue the lily-white city contracts they enjoyed. Maynard was determined to bring action to Affirmative Action, setting the model for the nation. The significant minority participation in the construction of the world's largest airport, finished on time and under budget, was, and is, a testament to his courage and leadership. Thousands of words have been written about his years as mayor, dealing with all the challenges and goals. He would say years later that his administration had to deal with "exaggerated black expectations, and exaggerated white anxiety."

His presence was undeniable. Often described as America's most eloquent mayor, Maynard carried confidence not only in himself, but in his beloved city of Atlanta. And he never, ever failed to recognize family publicly or privately. To me, he was a brother-in-law, always quick with a smile and croon. With everything else, he was blessed with a smooth, charismatic voice. We had a great relationship and he served as my best man when I married Birnur. He would come to Melody and Orman's birthday parties and always find time to literally play with them, if only a few minutes, especially Orman, he was Maynard's good buddy. And, a couple years after his death I walked his daughter, Valerie Amanda, down the aisle in her wedding.

I got the call from my brother, Robert, on Saturday morning. Maynard had suffered a heart attack minutes after arriving at the airport in Washington D.C. It was a shock to all of us. Grieving is tough enough but to be immersed in the energy and attention of the entire city, is not something you are prepared for. Reporters camped out at the end of the street, family coming and going, every TV channel running reports and obituaries. Valerie held up as best she could with her two daughters, "VA" and Alexandra. That Monday evening she called and we talked a few minutes. She was weak and quite distressed, but knew she had to look after Maynard. Then, to my surprise, she asked if I would speak at his funeral on behalf of the Richardson family. I knew Maynard better than any other family member, but still, it was a heavy request. I was honored. Aside from my wife and children, it was the greatest honor I've known.

The funeral would be a huge event, thousands in the audience at the Civic Center, hundreds of thousands viewing on TV. The stage included speakers Coretta Scott King, Andrew Young, Rev. Joseph Lowery, Jesse Jackson, Congressman John Lewis, President Bill Clinton and a who's who of Black America in the audience. With all that, I really wasn't that intimidated, perhaps it was the shock we were all experiencing. I held Maynard in as high regard politically or socially as anyone there, and I knew he would have confidence in me. Perhaps I should have been intimidated; here I am a college drop-out about to honor the "most eloquent mayor in the country." But, I wasn't that worried about stumbling or grammar or freezing and forgetting what to say, I was afraid I wouldn't be adequate, that I would not add something he would appreciate, and my family would be proud of. It was a very intense week, not to mention the hectic environment at work with constant attention from colleagues, and understandably, their requests for access or comments from the family. But with Birnur's help, I tried to bring some words together.

The day of the funeral we all gathered at Valerie's, my brothers and sisters from Richmond and several relatives from Maynard's family. Most of us would ride in a procession of limousines, perhaps ten or so, with an escort of police vehicles and other personal cars. Melody was thirteen and she and Birnur's mother, Nur, joined us. Orman was seven and, as most of the young children of family, stayed at the house. I wish he had joined us, and he does too, but the family agreed that given the space and seating, and a four hour program, the younger cousins should stay together at home. I regret that, because he deserves a memory of that tremendous goodbye to his uncle, his buddy.

Everything was live on local TV, as well as on C-SPAN. Helicopters flew above and followed the stream of vehicles down the freeway the short distance to downtown and through the streets to the Civic Center. Valerie was escorted in by President Bill Clinton, surrounded by other dignitaries and family. Many friends who had worked in Maynard's administration helped to orchestrate the program which included singers and choirs. There were corporate leaders from Delta Airlines and Coca-Cola. After two hours, and words from the mayor, a governor and a president, it was my time. I knew half the people on that stage, both from personal meetings as well as working in TV, and they knew I was Valerie's brother, however, the great vast majority in the crowd and the TV audience would learn for the first time. And, like hundreds of times before in my forty-five years, I knew that floating behind all those eyes was the same thought; "Damn, that is the whitest brother I've ever seen." It was not something that bothered me necessarily, I wasn't nervous but it is a strange and rare dynamic when a speaker can feel exactly what everyone in the audience is thinking, if only for the first few moments. It was different but not all that unusual, only in the scale of it. I had been accustomed to those kinds of thoughts for years, just not that volume at one time. The bright lights almost blinding, it felt like being in a giant cave, cornered. Here, at a significant point in black history, my history, might have seemed poignant. But black I am, and I made it a point to acknowledge Mrs. King first, then the president, then the mayor and others. My remarks were not the most eloquent, nor ebullient praises of a great leader as a few before me, I simply tried to express my thoughts about a good human being, a good man. I would like to think that when I walked off stage they were not thinking I was the whitest brother, but just the brother-in-law of a great mayor.

Moscow 1991. My host, Vladimir,
gave me one of his officer uniforms. Quite the comrade.

The cameraman; eyes without a face. With my partner Bill Liss,
who would always give me credit on the air.

Going aboard for a story about mid-flight fueling of the F-22 fighter jet.

End of the Soviet Union. The new Russian flag flies in Red Square, Dec. 1991.

The beautiful capital of three empires, Istanbul.

Birnur and her mother in front of the last great Ottoman palace,
'Dolmabache'.

My 35th birthday with Birnur and Melody on the Ageean coast in Turkey.

Our kids have a rich heritage; Afro-American Turks. In front of the fifteen-hundred year old Aya Sofya. Once the capital of Christendom, now a mosque and museum.

A Roman amphitheater in the foreground, and the castle of St. Johns knights in the distance, Bodrum is truly amazing.

A beautiful evening in 2006. The next day I ruptured my achilles.

Europe meets Asia, on the Bosphorus. My last trip to Istanbul in 2010.

With my cousins, Bill (left) and Walter Greene in 2016.

Melody, Orman, myself and Birnur, Christmas 2016.

Thirteen

The hills in Smoke Rise are long and steep in some areas, covered by tall hardwoods and manicured lawns, they give a Saturday morning jogger a serene comfort while the sweat builds and you lose yourself in pensive, or lazy, thoughts. Almost every weekend I ran a course of about five miles throughout my neighborhood in northeast Dekalb County. There were a few regulars I would see that had the same schedule who would nod in passing, acknowledging mutual respect for trekking this hilly area a few miles outside the perimeter highway around Atlanta. In my late forties, I would more often walk the hills than not, gazing at the tops of trees that would catch the early sunlight. The morning dew would also catch the sunlight as it, almost imperceptibly, washed it from the lawns and rooftops. Besides the sound and sensation of my steps, and my breaths, my company was the radio in my headphones. To this day, when I hear the opening theme of 'weekend addition' on NPR I feel melancholy for those brisk early jogs.

One cold morning in March 2007, I found that even walking those hills seemed to make me feel like I was in my eighties; my legs would not do the work required without stopping every few yards. However, I didn't give it much thought because I had only recently been given the OK to run again. For the previous five months, I had slowly recuperated from a ruptured Achilles tendon, the result of playing basketball with men half my age, and now, sought to fight back to that point of delusional confidence. I pushed through and up like any athlete who believes the mantra "no pain no gain," having faith in my large and muscular thighs thirty years after running and jumping in competition. That day, I would run only a little of my remaining distance, feeling the ache reach beyond my thighs into my waist. It was normal, it's to be expected, I thought to myself. After not running for almost six months that kind of thing happens. So, I worked it off as they say, fighting a sense of being strapped around my waist and legs in bands of aching weakness.

In the next few weeks, the notion that it was simply a stage in my recovery was the last thing I believed. I started to feel other pains just making normal movements. If I crossed my arms, my shoulders would feel stretched, like the feeling you get behind your knees when you try to touch your toes. I would wrestle with my eleven-year-old son, Orman, on the floor and find I wasn't able to do a single pushup. The year before, I could do a handstand from a squatting position, something Orman would marvel at. Now, I even noticed the effort of simply getting up from the floor was different. Something was wrong.

I saw my doctor and described the strange weakness and the tight feeling in my muscles. "Something is not right, I don't know, but something is not right," I said. "We'll see, could be something, could be not," he told me. Dr. Curry was that way, not an alarmist about things. He had been my primary-care physician for almost ten years and had a very easygoing nature. "Let's get some blood, see if we find something odd," he said. He said he wasn't sure what it could be, that there was no need to speculate a lot at this point. He shook my hand and casually walked out saying he'd be in touch. I left with the same casualness, assuming perhaps a type of virus or flu or something. I headed back to work and didn't much think about it. It was mild and sunny and I thought of Miami. My daughter, Melody, and I would be visiting the Univ. of Miami in a couple weeks as she began considering colleges. I went about things without much notice unless I was climbing stairs or walked for a prolonged time. This was the start.

"You have something called Polymyositis, it's a serious disorder." Basically, those were the first words I heard from Dr. Zelman, the rheumatologist from Kaiser, my insurance company. He would be treating me for this thing, polymyositis. He stood beside my hospital bed and told me the biopsy they had taken from my right thigh was consistent with the autoimmune disease that wills your own body to attack the muscles, breaking down your strength. It is usually confined to the proximal muscles, those near the torso, the muscles above my elbows, above my knees, as well as the shoulders, back and stomach. "There is no cure yet, but we can treat it pretty well with steroids like prednisone and other immunosuppressant drugs," he said. I was not too alarmed, but I understood there would be more to this than a couple days in the hospital. I was able to walk without much effort, and one would hardly think there was anything at all wrong with me. Some colleagues, and my sister Ruth, had noticed a loss of weight and a more hollow look to the eyes, but no notice of a significant change in my movement. I would not be too apparent fighting the ache and effort to rise from chairs and walk.

At first, I was put on a whopping 60mg of prednisone a day, although my strength was far from gone at that point. My impression, at that time, was that my weakness would not get much worse; that this was what I would deal with until it turned around. The prednisone was very tough though, it left me feeling very fatigued. I would sometimes sweat for no reason and feel as though my energy was zapped. It would eventually cause my blood pressure to rise, but otherwise I was relatively strong. I saw a doctor at Emory for a second opinion and she agreed with the diagnosis, but assured me that "there are a lot of worse things you could have." Despite Dr. Zelman not feeling it was necessary at that point, and noting it was "patient driven", I pushed for approval to visit Johns Hopkins in Baltimore. They have one of the few Myositis centers in the country and top doctors in the field. There, I saw one of the foremost experts, Dr. Lisa Christopher-Stine. Dr. Stine, a small woman in her mid-thirties with a warm smile, knew about as much as one could know about my condition. She expressed confidence that I would be able to treat and control this, but she told me it was progressive and we have to find the right med or combination of meds. "There is a whole mountain of drugs we can try, right now we are up here and we have all this as possibility." She held her hands up and formed the shape of a pyramid while she assured us. Birnur and I left feeling better about things, mostly impressed by the warm and smart young doctor. We spent the next day site seeing around Baltimore and I remember the painful walks we took. I didn't want to complain much to Birnur and pushed through, but it was at times after ten or fifteen minutes without rest, an agonizing, disheartening tour.

Back in Atlanta, I continued to see Dr. Zelman who, while seeming to do his best, had very little experience with my condition. He would sometimes come to our brief meetings with photocopy pages of medical literature about treatments, as if to show he was not just guessing. Although it didn't appear to be something they were overly worried about, when doctors literally shrug their shoulders it's not very comforting. Still, he too was assuring that, while it could take time, it was something I could manage. I remember once he looked at me all wide-eyed and leaned in with an almost whisper and said, "At least you don't have cancer." I thought to myself, "That was weird." It was another one of those moments that, while on the positive side, seemed odd. It seemed the doctors were only able to give me the same cliché my friends might say . . . "It could be worse" or "at least you can still use your hands." Over the years, I found that term began to annoy me. I didn't resent the intent of the person saying it. I understand why we say that to each other. I just noticed that I had never heard it from someone who had it worse, credibility in a way. This was one of the unreasonable jealousies I developed, like people doing the most mundane and unconscious movements, such as walking.

Birnur and I continued the visits and the blood tests, and I tried to assure my son, Orman, that I wouldn't be this way too long. "How long do you think before you are better, dad?" he said to me one night as I put him to bed. "Not too long, probably by my birthday in August," I said. At ten years old, the two months till August was no short time. Orman had seen me fall once or twice, not badly, but in a slow-motion almost comic manner. We were still able to throw the football and play bat, and shoot a few hoops, but I was not myself. My birthday came and I had to give him a new timeline to keep, "I think it will be alright on your birthday in May." He gave me a look that said he could wait, but also with disappointment and fear that we both pushed aside.

It was, to say the least, not to be pushed aside. This strange weakness was so strange indeed. A weakness of the muscles that might maintain me to some point in movement and then progress to total failure. It was becoming difficult to get up from chairs and go up steps, difficult to turn in bed or dress myself. That fall, I tried to go back to work. I couldn't handle anything physical with the camera so I worked as an editor. Then in October, my urologist told me my Prostate-specific antigen test or PSA was high and believed I should have a biopsy, which came back positive. I am fortunate that it was caught early. I told Dr. Stine at Hopkins and she seemed mildly thrilled. She said they believed that Myositis is probably triggered by a trauma, like my Achilles rupture, or they believed, a tumor or cancer that would flip the controls on the immune system. She said it was a good possibility that once the cancer was treated, the Myositis would follow in remission. One more weird thing to hear. I could imagine Dr. Zelman whispering "at least it will end the Myositis."

The treatment for the prostate was radiation therapy. It was a brutal period of trips to the hospital every day for five weeks. Every day, Birnur, after having been up since 2:30 am., would come home from work, a twenty-minute drive, pick me up then drive me to Northside Hospital, another twenty minutes. I could walk fairly well at that point, but it was still slow and measured. Inside, Birnur would help me change into a gown and go into the room for a one minute session of treatment then back to get dressed and back to the car. It was the kind of burden that would define our lives for five or six long years, struggling to get me in and out of chairs and cars, in and out of doctor appointments. The never ending anxiety over any travel; the burden on Birnur to load my chair, will I have help in and out of the car, what will the bathroom situation be like, will it be raining, are there steps . . . ARE THERE STEPS? It was fucked up, this thing, Polymyositis.

Fortunately, the treatment, knock on wood, was successful on the cancer, but not the Myositis. The weakness seemed to get better and worse on its own terms. I would get better for a few months, then for no discernible reason get worse for a few months. After a couple years, my walking was now obvious to everyone, a gangly gait, swinging my hips and arms, my fingers reaching for nonexistent support. The most important consideration was where I stepped. Any incline or decline, or heaven forbid an unseen ridge or bump that would cause my knee to bend even the slightest, would send me down. I went down more than a few times, luckily most times inside. It was, and is, a terrifying moment. For a split second, you think "oh shit," then the next split second a strange wave rushes over you I cannot describe other than a warm fear. Falling is scary for everyone but because I didn't have any arm strength there was no way to break the fall, no ability to recover or save myself. Falling for me meant a dead drop, like I fainted, only different, I was fully conscious each split second. It is depressing to measure the level of stress it had on me over the years, fearing each and every day a fall doing the most basic activity, whether using the bathroom or showering, getting the milk from the refrigerator, or just getting out of bed, my concentration had to be there.

The treatments ranged from pills such as Methotrexate, Imuran, Prednisone, low dose Naltrexone to infusion trials of Rituximab, Cytoxin, Acthar, and Ivig, to even trying plasmapheresis. Plasmapheresis is somewhat like dialysis, in that it removes the blood and then filters the plasma where the antibodies exist, which are then replaced with a saline-based solution. Birnur's mom had heard that it was being used in Multiple Sclerosis patients in Europe. It was determined at Johns Hopkins that I had a very unusual antibody present in the blood. It would require a surgical procedure to install a catheter in an artery where the nurse could easily attach the 'in and out' tubes. There was one visit for the preparation and overview then another for the surgical implant, then followed by three days a week for two weeks, then a week off and repeated. I didn't really feel a great improvement and it seemed, like other things, it would not be the key to recovery.

In 2010, I began to see Dr. Waltuck at Emory, and a year later a neurologist, Dr. Kennedy. They too can not understand my case but are very smart and never allow me to feel defeat. Although I don't see Dr. Christopher at Hopkins but every year or so, she remains in touch via emails and calls. I am one of her few "special" cases, one of only eighty-eight people in the world with my particular profile. All three doctors have become my friends, of sort, seeming to take a little extra interest and care as we all learn from my ordeal. Very few people, unless in the medical field, have heard of Polymyositis. The average person is, as was I, totally clueless about it. There is a lot of information available on the internet and other sources, but unless a celebrity of some kind must face it, there is really no way people would know about it. After a couple of years, my "stump speech" about Myositis became so routine I would sometimes wonder afterwards if I had already given it to that person. And, after a couple years my knowledge about it seemed to reach a peak. Internet searches, Myositis blogs and forums, would reveal little new in medicine or treatments, just the anecdotal surprises.

One surprise seems to hold valid promise to some. One day in early 2010, I was listening to a show called Radio Lab. They select various themes and do two or three unusual or little-known stories related to the theme. They were talking about parasites, things that live off other things, sometimes overtly and sometimes completely undetected. In one story, they spoke with a man in England named Jasper Lawrence, who talked about his debilitating allergies and the futile traditional approaches he had been through. He said he had heard about the role of parasites in humans on a BBC documentary and became obsessed with the notion that hookworms might be his answer. The documentary followed ideas that modern, or so-called advanced western societies, were unwittingly ridding us of beneficial bacteria or "parasites," an idea that is growing in scientific circles around the world. It is called the hygiene effect, the notion that we have cleansed ourselves too well, eliminating organisms that have evolved within, and with us, over thousands of years that have consequently become a normal key to proper immune development and regulation. It seems that as worms adapted to human immune systems, some say by releasing some sort of an enzyme, they prevent the immune system from over reacting; creating auto-immune disorders. Lawrence pointed out the virtual absence of many such disorders in "Third World" nations, disorders that have become epidemic in America. He described his journey to "infect" himself with the worms, which were not available from any lab or medical facility. So, it would have to happen by way of villages in sub-Saharan Africa.

The worms are contracted, typically through the foot, in areas where people would defecate. The feces serve as the conduit of larvae from the human host. Hookworm larvae are able to crawl up to six feet, reaching human feet not realizing the exposure. Lawrence trampled through many areas villagers had used as latrines. He claimed after about six months his allergies all but disappeared. It was compelling, and I researched as best I could the theory of this "hygiene effect."

We have all heard the saying, "you have to eat a little dirt before you die," maybe there is reason for it. It is the exposure to small amounts of dirt or germs, that actually allow the body to develop the resistance, the immunity to it. It is basically how a vaccination works. Perhaps, we have created an environment absent of some of the germs or parasites that are beneficial, causing the body to overreact to normal things. But some believe it is the outrageous levels of toxins in western society that is the culprit. There are chemicals soaking our lives in everything from the food chain, to cleaning products, to even our clothes and furniture. My guess is it is likely both, but while I couldn't remove myself from most of the toxins, maybe I could expose myself to the "good" parasites. Hookworms, in small amounts are not a danger, not even to people not necessarily needing treatment, the CDC even says so. Of course constant exposure and a growing presence is another issue. Right now, researchers in many countries are looking into this. I was told I would be getting around 50-70 worms, still an experimental dose, to see what dose is effective while not causing detrimental effects. The worms usually survive in your intestines for one and a half to two years. It did not sound like a big deal, considering the possible benefit.

I talked with my doctors, and while they reacted with the raised eyebrows I saw in friends, they did not automatically reject it. They certainly could not officially recommend it, but given my case they seemed curious and took a kind of go-for-it position, albeit informally. Going for it though, was in my hands. I contacted the company Lawrence had established in England to produce the worms. But, it was forbidden by the FDA to send them through the mail to America. I could understand the reason behind that, just a categorical issue. However, I can imagine the powerful pharmaceutical industry has such a lock on the medical industrial complex, it is impossible they would allow something as convenient as the product of shit to be an answer to some of ailments that they make millions on pushing toxic immunosuppressant chemicals.

That, however, was not the case with mailing it to Turkey. We had already planned to visit in the summer, so I met the worms in Istanbul. I had them mailed to our good friend, Meral, who is a Ph.D., in fact a leading government researcher at the time on the "bird flu," a global concern then. She was very familiar with my history and had talked with several colleagues about the use of parasites. They were aware of their application in various countries, particularly in China, but could not give any empirical guidance. That visit to Turkey was spent basically in the apartment home of Birnur's brother Onur. Getting around in Istanbul was terribly tough. There is no "Turks with Disability Act." Only in the very newest developments, and sometimes not there, are there ramps or access to buildings. Even in Onur's building, a very new and fashionable residence, there was only one way to enter the building without using steps, from the parking garage. And, that seemed almost coincidence, not an actual plan for the disabled. It was so unfortunate because I could not visit most of our friends, even those with elevators, because I could not get to the elevators. It would require at least two men to lift me, in the chair, up the steps or over curbs. It really opened my eyes about the incredible hardships disabled people face all over the world.

The hookworms came in a very plain brown envelope, in a vial of fluid half the size of a small thimble. Barely visible to the naked eye, in the right light, at the right angle, I glimpsed the thirty or so helminthes wiggling in search of a host. With Meral, who brought them, Birnur, and my son, Orman, holding a video camera, I followed the directions to remove and apply my new guest. It was simply a matter of extracting the fluid with a small tube, squeezing it out on a patch, which I applied to the soft skin on the inside of my bicep. After an hour or so, I could feel the itch and sting of their entry, at times annoying. It was not painful at all, just the irritating sting of a mosquito, nine or ten near the same spot. This lasted a couple of hours, and the next day I could see a few red spots on the skin. The only other effect I felt was a few days of diarrhea about two weeks later. Diarrhea is bad enough for anyone healthy but for me it was a struggle, like any other movement, dealing with the effort to get to and on the toilet.

This kind of thing really makes some people squeamish, the thought of worms invading their body. I had mentioned to many people I was planning this, most of whom reacted with "are you serious?" Knowing the worms may only live a couple years, I was told if they helped, another dose could be used. The company that provided them was willing to defer any payment until they proved to be helpful. They had had good evidence that it was helpful in several conditions, such as Crohn's disease, but no experience with Myositis. They felt it only ethical not to charge, other than delivery for the dose. That, and their knowledgeable, caring demeanor on the phone over several weeks prior to my decision, gave me the trust I needed. I didn't get better in that next year, but I definitely did not get worse. I pretty much maintained an operating level of strength, able to get out of our car (tall SUV) and manage small curbs and steps. I also tried an on and off period of the IVIG, seeing if I could discern any difference, but noticed no changes. After two years I began to get weaker and I cannot be sure if it did not help. I had learned over a few years that this problem seems to act in waves or cycles. I tried the worms again, but after a year there was no change. I still hold hope, maybe I will give it another try, I don't know. I do believe there is something to the parasite therapy; it is just a matter of time to determine the effective methods or dose for a given disease.

Fourteen

For years now, the test of my will has to be met day by day. I was told I need to get all the assistive devices: chairs and lifts and accessible vans, etc., but my heart was afraid. I know there are thousands of people who have, however difficult, accepted the degree to which they are invalid, but I simply cannot just one day say "OK, I'm sitting down and that's it, I won't try again, I give up." Unless the effort becomes literally impossible, I have to keep making it happen myself, until the Myositis quits, hopefully. The strain on Birnur has been the worse; it reached the point where loading the chair and helping me was unsustainable. She injured her back severely, helping me; and I could not put her through it any longer. Ultimately a van became necessary, and I must concede it has made so much of a difference that my stress is half the level of a year ago, a night and day change for our day-to-day life. In early spring of 2014, I fell while entering the bathroom. I was wearing a new pair of socks and when they met the smooth marble floor I lost my support. Fortunately, I fell outside the bathroom onto carpet but I landed squarely on my knee which jammed my leg into my hip. I went to the emergency room and had X-rays which did not show any dislocation or break. There was tremendous pain I had not felt since my Achilles injury. The pain prevented me from standing for many months and when the pain was gone so was my ability to stand without support from Orman. It has remained this way and life is, at least for now, in a chair. I have been able to maintain my freedom through the van, which I'm able to drive from the chair. I have been able to go virtually anywhere in public, only the occasional home that has multiple steps to enter have been an issue.

One thing that has been consistent in my life is music. It has held my hand through every phase or stage, every laughter and tear, and I enjoy virtually any genre. I never learned to play an instrument, though I did try once in my thirties to play piano, but I have always felt an emotional tie to melodies and rhythm. Lately in life, it has meant even more, always embracing my spirit, always positive. It doesn't just touch a sentimental cord for "the old days," but music to me, at its core, is so hopeful. Even if it seems sad or 'the Blues,' the expression of the music itself conveys hope. I find particular beauty in Brazilian music, whether samba or bossa nova or modern popular, it has been my 'go to' place for comfort, for a happy hope.

One feeling music can't quite reach though is laughter. I have always enjoyed humor and wit, and fortunately, my brother Bobby, who is the king of comedy in the family, calls me at least every other day and we often find ourselves laughing to the point of tears. He actually worked in stand-up for a few years but life and family have a way of stealing. He will take almost any event or personality and we will have a whole skit written in a few minutes. One of the stories that has always been a family heirloom is when he was a kid and accidentally damaged my dad's brand new car. It was spring 1974, my dad had just bought a brand new 74 Chevrolet Caprice Classic. The first absolutely new car he had ever owned. He would wipe that car every day, parking it in the shade, buffing the already spotless chrome and wiping the fashionable landau vinyl roof. He would not drive it to work yet, at that point dad had a small Ford Pinto the city provided.

One day, my grandfather, a neighbor, myself and Bobby, who was about eight, were out in the yard enjoying the weather. The old men were talking about how short ten years is, (I guess it is when you reach your eighties), while Bobby was playing with a tire iron, or some call a crow bar. He was digging up dirt and creating divots in the yard. My grandfather had asked him to stop a couple times and then firmly demanded he stop. "Boy, put that thing down, I'm not telling you again!" Bobby sighed and swung his head down and around. He took the tire iron in his hands and decided to throw it to the back of the yard. When he swung and released it the curved end of the iron held on just long enough to hook the release to the inside. That bar flipped and flew right at our dad's brand new car. Wham, bop, bam! The crow bar walked all over the front fender and dropped with a thud, just like Bobby's heart. My granddad, the neighbor, myself, our jaws dropped. Bobby started hopping around like he was on fire, not knowing whether to pick up the bar or touch the car or just pretend nothing happened. My father would be another hour before he got home and we all stood around in disbelief, except Bobby. He paced the yard and driveway, in and out of the house with an uncanny resemblance to my dad as he walked and looked at the ground. It became overwhelming and he could only escape the anxiety, the terror, by escaping his thoughts completely. He went inside and actually went to sleep; he consciously went unconscious, passed out. Talk about pressure. For years Bobby told the story in hilarious fashion, mimicking his slow-motion lurch for the bar as it whipped toward the car, the 'conversation' it had with the right front fender, and the snap awakening when my dad returned. Long and funny story but suffice to say Bobby labored in the yard till he was 34.

Comic relief is so valuable in life. It releases, if only a short while, the weight of physical or emotional burden we all must endure at times. Humor has always been the character of our family, for many black families I suppose, and it has always provided a type of joyous perspective, that so much in life really is how you look at it, and that laughter can be such good medicine.

Like all of life can trigger, dreams have been derived from my condition, though none recurring. They typically play out in some fashion of me regaining my ability to walk. They might sometimes speak about other problems, but I am almost invariably walking in them. When I was very young, maybe five or six, I had a recurring dream. It was actually the first dreams I remember. In it, my family is holding me up against our house and I am being painted over, painted onto the house, purple. I would be stuck on the side of the house under purple paint. I can see the mind working here, but purple I cannot understand. With Myositis, there has been one dream that, while it never repeated, has been a guidepost. It happened about two years into this maze, and I will always see it as an epiphany. It was Maynard, my sister Valerie's late husband. Maynard had died about five years earlier and he came to me in the dream. It was very short but very clear. With his broad smile and confident nature, he looked at me and said in such classic Maynard fashion "Brother, don't worry 'bout it, everything's gonna be fine. Three things . . . Breathe, Believe and Behave." That was it . . . a smile, a nod, and a few words. When I woke it was like I dreamt the route to a secret treasure. It was like the perfect words from the Buddha, words to live by, for life in general. Breathe, don't panic, stay focused and calm. It is a core consideration in meditation. Believe, have that "faith," know you can and will sustain yourself. And Behave, do the things you should and don't do the things you should not. I try to hear those words, and listen to them, as I and Birnur and Melody and Orman live with this.

Polymyositis is rare in and of itself; fewer than ten in a million. However, the profile I presented, with the unknown antibodies and the lack of response to treatments, is seen in maybe one in ten million. One in ten million, thank you very much. A very disturbing notion that isn't necessarily strange or incongruous as simply fucked up. The quizzical, sometimes sympathetic gaze of others asking themselves and me, "What's the deal with you," was not so new . . . that same familiar feeling from my childhood. I remember the anxiety and, to an extent, the unwarranted shame I felt when I was ten. And, I remember blaming Man and God for the neglect. But it is not neglect, just chance. Here I am again, in a place where virtually no one else lives, feeling special yet damned at the same time. After seeing so much over the years, I think I understand the value of religion. Not it's truth necessarily, or the ultimate answer, but the purpose of faith. While I don't believe religion is necessary, I believe faith is. That may sound like a contradiction but only if you see faith as a product of religion. I tend to see it the other way around. The trek of a hundred fifty thousand years has demanded a belief or faith in this sojourn of life. Hope is not enough, we must believe in an ultimate justice, because we have learned it is not a guarantee in this life. So faith is simply hope, empowered by belief. Enter religion. In the Bible, Pilate told Jesus before his crucifixion that he had power to release him. Jesus said to him he had no power but what was given from above, and " therefore he that delivered me unto thee hath the greater sin." Jesus believed God betrayed him... until resurrection. Faith, in "everlasting life" -through Jesus- is the story one religion provides power to hope, thus belief, or faith, when life seems to betray us.

I will say at this point I am agnostic. I certainly believe, given life itself, that anything one can imagine is possible in the universe, so why not a "creator" or Aristotle's "Prime Mover." I simply don't believe it exists in the way portrayed by men thousands of years ago. I do believe our own minds have power we don't grasp, if only over our own bodies and happiness. Perhaps, that is my faith. In religion, I guess I believe like the Dalai Lama; "The only true religion consists of having a good heart." "It's in the Lord's hands now, ain't no use in worrying about it," my mother would say at times. She had a way of curing uncertainty, for herself at least, through faith. And it was not lost on her children that things would be ok, that one only needs faith. It was something I had as a kid, but not just religious, I had a faith in myself. I believed, as arduous as it might be that I was capable, mentally and physically of handling almost anything. The burden, then, was at least manageable. A ten-year-old, if only of naiveté, can escape from the public and find a curtain to pull, a shadow from the energy of others. Today, it is inescapable. There is never a moment I forget what I face, never a moment I can feel naïve. Strangely, I do feel the same faith in myself I had as a kid. It battles, and defeats mostly, the despondency that tries to overwhelm me. There is a voice in my head that says it will be all right, perhaps the echo of my mother embracing me through a fever, or allaying my fears about the first day of school. However, this time, the battle is not with an external challenge but an internal one. And again, a foe that, while not necessarily a monstrous threat, hardly anyone else knows. But, I do know as well that faith in yourself is the key, that like flying a kite, life can at times soar with thrill and then dip with great risk; it can be monotonous and yet still rewarding. And like the kite, you never let go, you learn how to fly it, and develop faith in your ability to do so.

In the summer of 2016, I went back up to Johns Hopkins to visit Dr. Christopher. My cpk enzymes had been going down consistently (which is good) and she wanted to do a full body MRI. She wanted to see how much inflammation there was, and to see generally how I looked. She was also curious because in the summer of 2015 I had a form of stem cell therapy. It was something new that a few clinics around the country were trying. It is still in the trial stages so insurance doesn't cover it, and the medical community has mixed opinions about it. It is called Adipose stem cell therapy, stem cells taken from your own fat tissue. It seems stem cells in your body's fat remain locked in, still viable, but trapped in the fat unable to respond when the body needs it. So, doctors remove the fat tissue, put it in a centrifuge device of sort, extract the stem cells, then infuse them back into your body, sometimes with local injections as well. The hope being that the cells act as new help to the damaged muscle in my case. I went to a clinic near Orlando, Florida. The whole procedure, in and out, took about three hours. It was basically a mini liposuction. The doctor numbed an area on the rear of my waist and inserted a needle to draw a couple ounces of fat tissue. They extracted the stem cells, and with an IV, returned them to my body, free to seek out purpose. I was told it's unknown how long it could take to even see if it would help, six months, a year? And after a year I didn't feel much additional strength, so I can't say it helped, but I can't say it didn't, yet.

At Hopkins, Dr. Christopher wanted to do a genome study or "mapping" it's called. My case is one of so few I'm now considered actually a 'research' case. The National Institutes of Health agreed to do the study, which can take a month or so. They look for anything that suggests a link to something . . . other diseases, mutations, etc. They didn't find anything remarkable, or at least anything they believe, at this point, is connected. And, my full body MRI came back with little to no inflammation. Inflammation is one of the key markers of Myositis. Lack of it does not necessarily mean the absence of Myositis, there are molecular changes in the muscle as well, but it is a strong indication. "Maybe this thing has just burnt itself out" Dr. Christopher told me. It was all good news, perhaps this disease is in remission, perhaps gone altogether. Although, as has been the case for almost ten years, not the answer. But maybe it has burnt itself out, maybe I can climb out of this trap.

I will never really understand the impact it has had on my son, Orman. He has seen me slowly go from a dad that would wrestle and throw long football passes, to a man he had to literally pick up almost daily from a car or chair. All of his pre-teen and teen years, he would often have to join us where we went just to help me, not to mention the falls at home and all the extra work that slowly built as a result of my inabilities. He was ten years old when I ruptured my Achilles in Turkey. It was our vacation and Orman loved to play basketball. We were in Bodrum and there were several older guys (late teens early twenties) at the resort, including a young black player who played on the French national team. We would have friendly games that included Orman; he would hit three pointers and really impress them. One afternoon he asked if we could play. We were waiting on Birnur and her mom who had gone to have their hair done and even though I thought it was too hot I agreed and we went to the courts. I was doing pretty well playing against such younger men. Between the older man and his young son we were showing those scrubs how to do it.

At one point, I broke for a pass and immediately received the toss, and that's when the car hit me. Not a car actually, but I honestly thought a large heavy object had fallen on my ankle. There was a young man guarding me and he was right at my back but it was certainly more than his foot on me. I stopped and winced in pain as I limped from the court. We stopped the game and I hopped down to the side of the pool and sat. Sweating like crazy and in bad pain, I held my ankle for a while and slowly realized the extent of things. I noticed that on my right ankle I could feel the firm tight tendon at the back, from the heel upward. I felt no such tendon on my left. That was a moment I knew things would change. We went to the nurse onsite and she said we should go into town to the hospital. We hobbled onto a shuttle bus and went to the emergency room. There, a doctor confirmed the rupture and said he could repair it there and I would have a cast all the way up my leg to mid-thigh for six months. "Six months," I thought! It was unimaginable. We were scheduled to return to Istanbul the next day and the doctor said it could wait a day but two at most. So, I had the surgery at the American Hospital about 48 hours after the injury.

When I woke, it was the most excruciating pain I have ever endured. They gave me morphine, but it took close to half an hour to be any help. It was such a crazy pain. It was as if every motion of the handling of my ankle was being played out in a delayed sensation. I could feel the hands holding my heel and my arch and every grip or touch almost simultaneously. It was perhaps the drugs, but I have no doubt I was feeling what had happened. The next couple days were relatively comfortable, though a surprise when I showered. A middle-aged man washed me, an assistant of sorts who literally scrubbed patients unable to do so for themselves. That was strange, but I guess only because I had never considered that kind of thing was necessary. I spent three days at the hospital, including my birthday. It was my fiftieth, and that evening Nazli, Rengin's sister, and her husband Serhat brought a nice bottle of champagne and we laughed and talked to the point the nurse had to ask we keep it down. It was a private room, even flowers from the hospital director, who was American, and more room than needed. It was very nice and we all enjoyed the unusual setting for the good time. However, at one point I remarked that it was kind of eerie that it was my fiftieth birthday. Then I said something that has haunted me virtually every day since. "Man, my fiftieth birthday in the hospital, I hope this doesn't portend how it will be from here." It was one of those silly things you say to make conversation. But it was one of those things that human beings cannot believe is not related to an otherwise random course of events. Like my sister, Valerie, in 1966, believed that not picking up a fallen picture of her fiancée was why he was killed in Vietnam. It is as if I have caused all this shit myself. Even still, just as I was saved by an unknown teenager in 1971, I now have a hope, maybe belief, that an anonymous angel will intervene, again, in my risky condition.

The doctors think it is very likely the Myositis was triggered by the injury, and by that logic, the injury was because I played basketball. One evening a few years later, after Melody had gone to college at Howard University in Washington, D.C., we sat having dinner and watching TV just the three of us. It was discomforting to not have Melody around and I'm sure even more for Orman, but this evening he seemed especially quiet and bothered. Birnur and I tried to talk him into a little cheer but he remained quiet. We knew something was bothering him, perhaps school or a girl or the lack of friends that lived close by. Orman and Melody attended Paideia, a private school about a half hour away, and so just about all his classmates lived about that far. So we understood he may have felt unlucky and we tried to convince him his life was not so bad. After a while of nudging him, we felt a little upset that he just seemed to refuse to let us know what was bothering him. Then, he just leaned back on the couch and began to choke back tears. We didn't know what to think. "Orman, what's wrong sweetheart?" Birnur said softly. Orman told us through his tears that he felt bad because he believed that my illness was his fault, that if he hadn't insisted I play basketball that day we would not all be going through this.

As bad as things had been physically, emotionally this really put me on the floor. Birnur and I cried as well and assured him he should not feel that way. But, I understand how he could . . . those damn what ifs. I know it must be something that has run through his mind a thousand times as he watched me struggle over years that never found a cure for something "his fault." It breaks my heart. We were all enduring enough burden but the thought that our fifteen-year-old felt responsible was just cruel. BUT, I would not change a thing. I played basketball with my son, something I treasure, no one's fault. No regret. Sometimes God damn shit happens, with no justice. "God works in mysterious ways," and that, for some is justice. But justice does not mean fairness. Fairness, to me, is an equation of morality, a distinct human 'order,' with emotion often tipping the scale of justice. The problem is there is often overcorrection with emotion, which might allow revenge to stand in for justice. One of the beautiful things in Christianity, and perhaps other religions, is the virtue of forgiveness. What makes forgiveness divine? Is it justice?

Over the years I've heard about ideas that try to describe the universe, and the battle with the concept of infinity, kind of like God. They say fear is the absence of understanding; it's what we don't know that frightens us most. I think, therefore I am. I don't know, therefore I fear. The twentieth century was full of books about positive thinking, visualization, mind over matter, and good vibrations. The basic concept is that our minds can be much more if we train them to be, perhaps with meditation. I believe there is something to it; after all, it's pretty well-accepted that attitude is everything. I read a book a few years back called The Biology of Belief, by Bruce H. Lipton. He spent years studying and teaching cell biology. He described how human cells develop in response to their environment, as much if not more so than the genetics within them. Cells respond to signals from such things as trauma, toxins, disease, or even energy such as radio waves. He believes cells actually respond to thought, that thought has energy. Maybe it's why stress is so unhealthy. But, he thinks it happens on a subconscious level . . . attitude.

My doctors tell me there is no chance I will regain the full abilities I had, the muscle scar tissue and fat displacement is too significant, but, given the ambiguous and unique nature of my case, they say "go for it," work what is there, get aggressive with physical therapy. It is possible I may walk again, maybe even dance a little, who knows. If I can breathe, believe and behave. If I can know it's possible, I can keep it possible.

I do know some things. I do know I have an incredible wife who has endured struggle at my side a thousand moments, she has dedicated her energy for me, and I lack the words to express my appreciation. I know I have family and friends that will continue be there as well. I know as cliché as it sounds, if you have your health you have everything. However, not having health does not mean you have nothing. This experience has left me, in a way, with more mentally than it took physically. Philosophically, intellectually, and emotionally, I feel stronger. Perhaps, at least, my mind believes that, a form of coping. Coping, is probably what most of us do in life. We strive to cope or adapt to the quirks of our fate. Millions of times a day all over the world great tragedy and heartbreak befall the innocent. As well, humans realize great potential and wisdom that provide possibility to all our lives, individually and collectively. Is there a reason? It is perhaps the quintessential purpose of human life, to pursue the answers of how and why. Maybe the purpose and answer are one in the same. Why shit happens is because it should, for Man's ultimate good; it's simple evolution.